THE
TOASTMASTER GENERAL'S
FAVORITE JOKES:
Openings and Closings
for Speechmakers

The Toastmaster General's Favorite Jokes

OPENINGS
AND CLOSINGS
FOR
SPEECHMAKERS

by

George Jessel

CASTLE BOOKS

ACKNOWLEDGMENTS

My deep appreciation to
Elizabeth Cossa
and Jean Vermes
for their editorial
assistance.

Arrangement has been made to publish this edition by Castle Books,
a division of Book Sales Inc. of Secaucus, New Jersey

Manufactured in the United States of America

June — 1978

Contents

Part I

Effective Openings and Closings

Chapter 1

GETTING
STARTED

One of Don Knott's favorite routines is that of an inexperienced speaker, shaking with fear. In his nervousness he says all the wrong things, continually putting his trembling foot in his quivering mouth.

Panic at the thought of standing up on a dais in front of a large group of people is a perfectly normal reaction. The reason Don gets his laughs is because everyone recognizes an exaggeration of his own feelings at the thought of getting up and making a speech.

The Importance of Preparation

You can keep your fears and worries to a minimum by being well prepared. The opening of a speech should be thoroughly rehearsed ahead of time. During the middle of your talk, after you have gained some self-confidence and audience approval, you may be able to play it by ear; but you must have a plan for securing your listeners' attention at the start. There is nothing guaranteed to turn them off faster than hesitations like "er-uh-er," "I mean," "y'know," or "that is." They will sense your brain is idling and will let theirs drift likewise.

Let's assume you have chosen your subject and collected basic material from which to draw your speech. Since it is necessary to have an opening, a main body, and a closing, sort your notes into three such piles. Go over the material under the subject of "opening," and decide the kind of start you want to make. Write down on 3″ by 5″ or 5″ by 7″ cards the points you want to put across, plus some statements to arouse audience interest.

Local Color

To begin with, if you're away from home, be sure to remember exactly where you are. Spiro Agnew, accomplished public speaker though he is, once made this kind of boo-boo in the pressure of preelection oratory. He referred warmly to one midwestern town when he was actually in another.

Make a note of your locale on your first index card, and underscore it. Then work in some kind of complimentary reference to the location. Be sure to get that down in writing so it doesn't slip your mind.

Keep It Familiar

Whether or not you intend to use technical words and complicated explanations later on, it is best not to start that way, because you are likely to scare people off. Use plain English and familiar phrases, like the former president of the Association of American Railroads, Thomas M. Goodfellow, in a speech to a Rotary Club: "I'm going to talk about railroads, but don't become alarmed. I'm not going to saturate a crying towel with copious tears and try to wrap you in it."

The use of a recognizable expression like "crying towel" or any other immediately establishes you as a regular guy or gal.

Accentuate the Positive

Mr. Goodfellow's remarks illustrate another point that makes for an effective opening. He immediately established the fact that he was going to give his audience some positive information along with the negative. At a time when the news in the various media fills us with despair, we get pretty fed up with troublesome questions and welcome a few satisfying answers. With this in mind the president continued: "I can't talk about our alarming railroad situation—and I do mean alarming—without introducing some of the problems—in the beginning, at least. But I'll get to the positive side, without too much delay, and discuss a few of the proposed solutions."

If all you do is view with alarm, your audience will turn away in self-defense. Give them some hope, and they will bear with you.

Preview What's to Come

One way to arouse audience interest is to itemize briefly the highlights of the points you expect to make. Louise Bushnell, of the National Association of Manufacturers, in addressing an American Business Woman's Association meeting, listed the following three points at the start of her talk to tease her hearers into attention:

"Point number one. . . . What is the women's liberation movement? . . . what does it want?

"Point number two. . . . What has brought the movement about? What are some of the causes of the present outburst?

"Point three: Is there a solution? What can be worked out that is practical and fair?"

You will note that the points are presented in the form of questions to further set the people thinking about the subject.

Relate to the Audience

Miss Bushnell then followed her three points with another sentence that recognized the reactions of her listeners. Such a recognition of their probable emotions helped give them the feeling that here was somebody who understood them: "The very mention of the women's lib . . . those two words can bring color to pale cheeks, flashes to dull eyes, twitches to a silent body, and venom to a calm tone. . . ."

If you can project a taste of what's to follow by itemizing the points you want to make and then establish a rapport with the listeners, you, too, are well on your way to a successful speech.

Make Them Smile

There is nothing like a laugh to put people at ease. They will, I've found, pay more attention to a serious message if you lead them into it in a lighthearted vein.

At the National Defense Luncheon of the D.A.R., magazine editor Tom Anderson, not in the least intimidated by those ladies, began thus: "Mrs. Jones, President General, my favorite Congressman—Congressman Rarick—honored guests, ladies and gentlemen, my wife has made me well aware of the many vital subjects you ladies are involved in. I can't possibly cover them all today. I feel sorta like a mosquito at a nudist camp. I know what I ought to do, but I hardly know how to begin."

When General Austin W. Betts, of the U.S. Army's Department of Research and Development, wanted to defend the ties between R&D and the universities, he began with a humorous comparison: "The situation reminds me of the letter Mark Twain once received from a friend. In the letter the friend complained how bad off he was—he had an earache and a toothache at the same time! What could be worse? Mr. Twain's reply was: rheumatism and St. Vitus's dance!"

Not exactly a boff, but not bad for a lead-in to a controversial subject. And the audience doesn't expect you, or a lieutenant general, to roll them in the aisles. All they want you to do is take the edge off the formality of a situation that has you standing up there in command and them sitting around at attention. Select a bit of humor that suits your subject, and work it into your introductory remarks so that it fits naturally and easily.

Illustrate Your Theme

A good way to arouse interest is to start out with a little illustration of your theme, as the Commissioner of Internal Revenue did in a speech entitled "The Tax Status of Exempt Organizations." Randolph Thrower led into this rather formidable subject by saying: "If the Internal Revenue Service had access to the Oracle at Delphi and could pose the question, 'What do you see ahead for the I.R.S. in the field of exempt organizations?' the answer would no doubt be a short and cryptic, 'Trouble.'"

Let's suppose, for instance, that your theme is "Evil is in the eye of the beholder." Then you might tell the story of the philosopher who stood at the gates of an ancient city greeting tourists. When one of them asked him, "What kind of people live in your city?" he countered, "What kind of people live in the city you came from?"

"Oh, they were very bad people," the traveler replied, "dishonest, immoral, and violent."

"That's the kind of people you'll find here," said the philosopher.

Then another tourist came along and asked the same question. When the philosopher asked him what kind of people live in the city he came from, he said, "Oh, they were very fine people—honest, moral, and decent."

"That's the kind of people you'll find here," the philosopher said.

Shake Them Up

A drowsy after-dinner audience can be awakened from its lethargy with a blunt statement that has a little shock value. In a speech at the State University of New York, Professor Paul L. Briand, Jr., gave them this treatment:

"America was born in violence, she lives in violence, and—unless she heeds the problems which beset her at home—she will die in violence. While I am standing here speaking to you, and before one minute has elapsed, a violent crime will have been committed in America. Before two and one half minutes have gone by, someone will be robbed; in six minutes, someone will be mugged; and before this speech is finished, someone will have been murdered somewhere in America."

The professor goes on to say that every day in this country one hundred Americans die on the highway and another one hundred die from smoking, and crimes of violence are increasing nine times faster than the population growth warrants.

This kind of introduction can be even more effective if the shocking statistics can be directly related to those present. A little research on the local incidence of crime, accidents, and illnesses might turn up some figures that would be a lot closer to home. Depending on your chosen subject, you might dig up some startling information on drug use, venereal disease, motorcycle accidents, firearm sales, pollution, or any of the other blights for which solutions must be found.

The Challenging Question

There are two kinds of questions with which you can begin your talk. One is known as the rhetorical question, which answers itself. Such a question was asked in the start of Professor Briand's speech:

"Our young people are up in arms (note my violent metaphor) because forty-two thousand of them have died in what they consider a senseless war in Southeast Asia. Why are they not also up in arms over the fifty-seven thousand Americans killed in one year in America in automobile accidents, half of them involving people their own age?"

As you can see, the question required no answer; it was made for oratorical effect.

The other kind of question would be a direct one, such as (to a young group), "How many of you have been involved in automobile or motorcycle accidents?" For an older group it could be, "How many of you have had children involved in motor accidents?"

Then you can go on to say, after you have had a show of hands, that in every family at least one of the children can be expected to be involved in such an accident before he reaches adulthood.

The question opening can be applied to almost any subject you want to discuss.

Sound Spontaneous

One of the secrets of successful public speaking is to sound as though you were talking off the cuff while at the same time knowing exactly what you intend to say. You can accomplish this right at the start by having the following key words and phrases typed on your reminder cards: (1) names of people and organizations related to the occasion, (2) colorful expressions you don't want to omit, (3) quotations and humorous references, and (4) dates and statistics, where needed.

In this way you won't overlook anything of importance, but you will be able to be flexible about the way you express yourself. An opening that is completely memorized makes you sound like a robot that's been programmed for speech, whereas one that is completely ad lib can be a disaster.

Be Ready for Anything

When you plan to attend any kind of function, even though you are not scheduled to speak, it is a wise precaution to have a few notations on index cards in your pocket. Some observations on an appropriate subject may come in very handy if you are called upon unexpectedly. This material will get you going, and all you need do is develop it. Your listeners will make allowances for your lack of formal preparation and will appreciate your ability to make some kind of coherent remarks on a moment's notice. If you can work in a good story, joke, or one-liner that suits the occasion, so much the better.

Chapter 2

CHALLENGING
SITUATIONS

There are a number of situations that may arise to disturb the opening of your speech. The experienced speaker, like myself, takes them in stride. But someone new to the game may be thrown by the noise of late arrivals or chatty ladies, the rattle of dishes, the unexpected absence of a table or lectern for props and notes, rumbling air conditioners or a bad mike, the presence of women in an audience presumed to be all male, or vice versa.

Then there are the audiences with which entertainers are all too familiar: the ones that sit on their hands; the ones that cough like seals; and those that—after too much food and drink—seem ready to fall asleep.

Overcoming Antagonism

Among the special problems that a speaker may have occasion to face is an antagonistic audience that sits there defying you with an "Okay, show me!" attitude.

Arthur Goldberg faced this situation during his unsuccessful run for governor of New York. True, he didn't win the governorship, but he did win over a less-than-enthusiastic group of Italian-Americans. With ethnic consciousness becoming so pronounced in recent years this problem could arise for almost anyone.

What Mr. Goldberg did was to identify with the Italians in their common feeling of resentment of a WASP-dominated society. He told of the preferential treatment of WASPs which he encountered as a young man starting out on his career. This indicated that he could sympathize with their desire to have their personal abilities

recognized and rewarded in spite of their ethnic background. He
also intimated, through his present eminence, the possibility for
others to reach equally high goals.

Establishing a Bond

Betty Friedan, of the National Organization for Women, in similar
circumstances also recognized the need to establish a bond with her
audience. She was facing a Southern group, among whom the men
were openly derisive. Ms. Friedan quickly wiped the sneers off the
men's faces with the following opening:

"Many people think men are the enemy in the movement I
represent. Man is not the enemy. He is the fellow victim. Why
should men die ten years earlier? . . . Why should man be saddled
with his masculine mystique, his image as tight-lipped, brutal,
crew-cut—not able to cry out for help?"

After that they were more receptive to her complaints about the
unsatisfactory position of women. With the right kind of opening
you can overcome seeming disinterest; after all, these people wouldn't
be there if they weren't at least curious about what you were going
to say.

Disarming Apathy

Perhaps even more of a challenge than possible antagonism is the
indication of boredom. If your listeners look up at you, heaving a
collective sigh that suggests, "So what?" because they think what
you're about to say will be routine, surprise them.

President Richard Nixon did this when he addressed the Twenty-
fifth Anniversary Session of the General Assembly of the United
Nations in 1970. Instead of giving them the "rah-rah" speech they
might have expected, he spoke in more down-to-earth fashion. After
a few sentences of tribute the President said:

"In celebrating an anniversary, there is a temptation to recount
the accomplishments of the past, to gloss over the difficulties of the
present, and to speak in optimistic or even extravagant terms about
our hopes for the future.

"This is too important a time and too important an occasion for
such an approach. The fate of more than three and a half billion
people today rests on the realism and candor with which we approach

the great issues of war and peace, of security and progress, in this world that together we call home.

"So I would like to speak with you today not ritualistically but realistically; not of impossible dreams, but of possible deeds."

Letting Them Down Easy

When you get in front of a group of people whom you are going to criticize, there is always the problem of softening the blow. One method of doing this is to present a hypothetical criticism that is so much tougher than the one you are eventually going to make that your later words will seem like a compliment in comparison. When Mayor A. J. Cervantes, of St. Louis, addressed the Federal Agency Review Workshop, he must have had this in mind:

"Gentlemen: It may sound like a bit of banter and playful needling for a mayor of one of the older, larger cities to initiate our discussion by stating: 'I have dreamed of the day when I would have the chief administrators of the federal grant program before me so that I could tell them exactly what I as a mayor think of their whole system of categorical grants.'

"I know some mayors who are so exasperated with the whole federal grant system that they would give up their own spleen and their cities' 'maximum feasible participation' programs to have the opportunity to meet in one room with you chief administrators of the Departments of Labor, Justice, Commerce, Defense, Agriculture, Transportation, H.E.W., H.U.D., and O.M.B. to tell you that as far as the core cities and their poverty peoples are concerned the grant system itself hasn't worked, isn't working, and can't possibly work.

"These mayors would tell you that the whole system of categorical grants is overregulated, undersupported, divisive, wasteful, frustrating, completely beyond the federal bureaucracy's capacities, substantially ineffective, in the long run subversive of the very federal system that gave it birth, and that the whole system must be radically altered from a revenue grant system to a revenue sharing system."

Cervantes's own statement, no matter how harsh, had to seem mild by comparison after that opening.

Another approach to the speech of criticism is the "This really isn't going to hurt you" gambit, used by Newton N. Minow when he was chairman of the F.C.C., addressing the National Association of Broadcasters:

"Thank you for this opportunity to meet with you today. This is my first public address since I took over my new job. When the New

Frontiersmen rode into town, I locked myself in my office to do my homework and get my feet wet. But apparently I haven't managed to stay out of hot water. I seem to have detected a certain nervous apprehension about what I might say or do when I emerged from that locked office for this, my maiden station break.

"First, let me begin by dispelling a rumor. I was not picked for this job because I regard myself as the fastest draw on the New Frontier."

Mr. Minow, as you may remember, then proceeded to criticize television programming in a way that started a discussion that is still going on and created the descriptive phrase "a vast wasteland."

On Camera

These days many talks are given over the communications media. On radio and television your audience is, to a great extent, an unknown quantity. They may love you or hate you or be yawning in your face. You don't know, and maybe it's just as well.

People of all generations, professions, backgrounds, and interests will be tuned in. Some may have turned you on intentionally; others may have you purely by accident. To reach such a broad mixture, your opening should have as wide an appeal as possible to common human motivations.

A.F.L.-C.I.O. President George Meany did this very well in one of his Labor Day broadcasts, when he did not confine himself, as might have been expected, to addressing union members:

"Traditionally, Labor Day is the day when the A.F.L.-C.I.O. not only looks to the future but reports to the American people on what steps American workers are planning to meet that future.

"So, today I want to report to you on Labor's number-one legislative goal—a goal not only for American workers and their families, but for all the American people: rich and poor; young and old; black and white; employed and unemployed.

"That goal is to upgrade America's standard of health; to establish a new and better system for delivering health care and health services to the people who need them.

"Now, we are not pretending to be doctors. We believe that only members of the medical profession should have any voice in medical decisions. Any other position would be silly.

"But while medical treatment is the doctor's business, health is everybody's business."

Of course, if you are addressing an audience in the flesh and the broadcast is only incidental, you can tie in your opening remarks more closely with your immediate audience and trust that the warmth of their response will communicate itself to outside listeners and viewers.

Mike Technique

Anyone who has ever spoken into a microphone for necessary amplification has had the experience of his opening sentences coming out muffled, distorted, or in one great blast of sound. This is because the average loudspeaker is able to handle a specific load of volume. When the signal is too great, it causes distortion; when you stand too close to the mike and your voice level is rather high, the sound will be muffled. The best position is with your face from six to twelve inches away from the mike. Stand too far away, and you won't be heard; stand too close, and you'll blast them out of their seats.

Remember that people absorb sound waves. You must speak more loudly to a capacity audience than to a small one.

Another way for your voice to get lost is for you to weave back and forth out of proper microphone range. You don't need to be stiff, but try not to get beyond a sixty-degree range to either side. The so-called lavaliere mike, which hangs around your neck, allows for more movement.

If you can possibly adjust the microphone ahead of time, do so. Adjustment of the mike during your speech can cause annoying bangs. Feedback can create a howling effect, and this is also preferably taken care of in advance, when the mike can be placed in proper position in relation to the loudspeakers.

When adjusting your position in relation to the microphone, you must also keep in mind the relation of your eyes to your notes. Position your notes so that you can stand the proper distance from the mike but at the same time read them conveniently. Avoid being on top of the notes so that each reference to them creates a bobbing effect or so far back from them that you have to crane and squint like a comic professor.

Laugh It Off

One way to combat certain difficulties at the start of your speech is to get the audience to join you in laughing them off. You could quiet any buzzing females in the crowd with the story of the explorer who had just returned from an African safari and was describing some of his adventures:

"I suddenly came upon a tribe of wild women who had no tongues," he said.

"What! No tongues?" exclaimed his listeners. "How in the world could they talk?"

"They couldn't," he explained. "That's what made them wild."

You might refer to clattering waiters or waitresses as "people who think money grows on trays."

Of late arrivals you might say, "Some people wake up and find themselves famous; others wake up and find themselves late."

Know What to Anticipate

It is a good idea, if feasible, to visit the hall where you are to speak a few days or a few hours ahead of time to look for possible sources of disturbance. Rehearsing your opening against the low sound of a radio can prepare you for ignoring potential distractions, such as street noises, humming air conditioners, or low-flying airplanes.

Many speakers carry a folding table in the trunk of the car to use in emergency, when a table or a lectern has not been provided. If your visual aids have been mislaid or forgotten, you'll just have to improvise without them.

Of course, if you're in the position of the man whose projectionist failed to show up when he was to give a talk keyed to a movie, you're really in trouble. If you can't dig up a substitute assistant in the crowd, you'll have to cancel, postpone, or suggest that they all catch the John Wayne Western down the street.

Chapter 3

SPECIAL
OCCASIONS

With the approach of the year 1976 all public speakers should be preparing for the flood of American bicentennial addresses they will be required to make. Every organization will be tying itself in with the anniversary of American independence, from the K. of C. to the Y.M.C.A., not to mention the J.D.L. and the N.A.A.C.P.

Aside from such anniversary oratory, the list of possible special-occasion addresses that may fall to your lot is varied: acknowledgments of honor, commencement addresses, conference speeches, inaugurations, opening ceremonies, and so on.

Acknowledgment of Honor

When you are being honored, it is customary to act modestly, express appreciation, and give credit to anyone else who may have contributed to your success. Lieutenant Colonel John H. Glenn, Jr., the first American astronaut hero, illustrated this when he was honored by being invited to address a joint meeting of Congress on behalf of himself and his fellow astronauts. He began:

"Mr. Speaker, Mr. President, members of the Congress, I am only too aware of the tremendous honor that is being shown us at this joint meeting of the Congress today. When I think of past meetings that involved heads of state and equally notable persons, I can only say I am most humble to know that you consider our efforts to be in the same class.

"This has been a great experience for all of us present and for all Americans, of course, and I am certainly glad to see that pride in our country and its accomplishments is not a thing of the past.

"I still get a hard-to-define feeling inside when the flag goes by—and I know that all of you do, too. Today as we rode up Pennsylvania Avenue from the White House and saw the tremendous outpouring of feeling on the part of so many thousands of our people I got this same feling all over again. Let us hope that none of us ever loses it."

He then went on to give credit to his parents, his parents-in-law, his children, his wife, everyone in the space program, his predecessors in earlier flights, and his companions on this. If you're going to give credit, you can't overlook anyone. Some speakers avoid that mishap by making a general statement like "I want to thank everyone who made my achievement possible," then including all those he can remember.

Anniversaries

The typical anniversary speech relates a past event with present realities and future possibilities. One starts out with a remembrance of the event being celebrated, follows its consequences over the intervening period, and expresses assurances for the years to come, before getting into the body of the talk.

Former Secretary General U Thant followed this plan in his San Francisco address on the United Nations' twenty-fifth anniversary:

"All of us who work in the United Nations are deeply grateful for the opportunity which the mayor and citizens of San Francisco have so generously given us to celebrate here the twenty-fifth anniversary of the signing of the Charter of the United Nations.

"To return to San Francisco is not only to come back to a beautiful, gracious, and civilized city; for us in the United Nations, it is also to return to the birthplace of the organization and to the congenial and forward-looking atmosphere in which the charter was created. Here we are reminded of the sense of dedication and urgency, tempered with realism and a vivid awareness of the horrors of war, which inspired the authors of the charter twenty-five years ago. If we have not yet succeeded in realizing their vision of a world at peace, we can still draw inspiration from the ideals and objectives which they set out with full support from the peoples. Our best tribute to them is to increase our efforts to strengthen the United Nations.

"This is the third time that the representatives of the United Nations—national ambassadors and international Secretariat—have come back to San Francisco to celebrate the signing of the charter.

"Fifteen years ago, in 1955, this ceremony took place in an atmosphere of cautious optimism at a time when the world seemed to be awakening from the tribulations of the postwar period and the long winter of the cold war.

"Five years ago we gathered again in a less happy mood to speak of a world in which new problems and new conflicts had dimmed the hopes of a just and peaceful world order—hopes encouraged by the great political emancipation of decolonization and the possibility of emancipation from drudgery made possible by science and technology. At that time, the United Nations itself was in the throes of a crisis which had arisen over the fundamental issue of financing peace-keeping operations.

"Now we meet again in a mood of uncertainty and anxiety, with only the knowledge that humanity is moving at an increasing speed in uncertain directions, and that time is running short. I hope we can make use of this opportunity, so generously afforded by the city of San Francisco, to turn the tables on the forces of doubt and gloom, in order to survey calmly, but with a sense of urgency, the course we must take in the next twenty-five years."

Commencements

Today's commencement address cannot be as high-flown and unrealistic as those of the past. In order to engage the attention of a youthful audience, you need to refer at once to something in which they are really interested. Richard White, a senior at Wabash College, knew how to appeal to his classmates when he began with a quote from a modern musical, rather than from some dry-as-dust philosopher:

" 'This is the Age of Aquarius, when peace will guide the planets and love shall steer the stars.' Today, this prophecy from the musical *Hair* sums up the feelings of many young Americans toward their society. Its appeal is especially strong among college students. For youth is asking basic questions about the goals and methods of our society in general and of education in particular."

He went on to describe some of the hypocrisy and brutality in our society which has turned off many of the young, while at the same time deploring the subculture of selfishness and drugs which has resulted.

You can criticize the mistakes of youth, after first prefacing them, as he does, by recognizing their legitimate gripes. The commencement speaker of today can't be hypercritical; neither can he have his head in the clouds.

Conferences

A succession of speeches at a conference can get pretty wearing after a while. To nudge your listeners into awareness after a big night at the bar or a heavy lunch in the dining room, you need a punchy beginning. Fred Smith seemed aware of this when he eased an Electrical Engineering conference into his subject with a reference to a familiar television program and added a quick twist that was guaranteed to wake them up.

"Among the strange phenomena of our time is the occasional integration into our lives of certain television shows. One of these has been *Mission: Impossible*. Week after week impossible problems are solved by impossible people with impossible talents using impossible methods, and obviously it is all impossibly simple when you know how. This apparently provides psychological compensation for people whose impossible personal and societal problems defy solution by any possible method. But the real attraction is the first few minutes of the strip, when a stentorian voice emerges from a tape recorder, bristling with authority and immeasurable wisdom, to define the problem at hand. It may involve the overthrow of an unacceptable government, or an arrangement to have a revolutionary group wipe itself out in an orgy of mistaken identity, or the defeat of a plot to eliminate the world's population with a mysterious gas—but the important thing is that it reduces earthshaking situations to crisp words of one syllable, issues unmistakable instructions such as never exist in the real world, and then the unseen genius cops out. 'If anything goes wrong,' he warns, 'forget you ever knew me.'

"Finally—and this is the clincher—the whole works blows up. This really rings a bell; a messiah appears with all the answers, sets about to reorder the world, issues marching orders, then dissolves in a puff of smoke, and we are left holding the bag. No wonder we can identify with the big blond hero. He is us."

This was a good lead-in to a talk about the big environmental problems of our time, about which we are constantly hearing and to which we are supposed to apply impossible solutions.

Inaugurations

We think of inaugural addresses in connection with the President of the United States, but many of us are inaugurated into offices that are less awesome, though equally important to ourselves. Although you should accept any office with a becoming expression of humility, you must also indicate your suitability for the job by presenting your personal concept of it.

Maceo T. Bowie, at his inauguration ceremony as president of Kennedy-King College in Chicago, took as his theme "Learn, Baby, Learn" and immediately expressed his individual viewpoint on what a community college should be and what it should not be:

"Chancellor Shabat, members of the Board of Trustees, distinguished guests, my friends, my colleagues and students of the Kennedy-King family, I accept with deep humility the charge just given me to serve as the first president of Kennedy-King College. Inherent in this charge is the responsibility to provide the best possible education for the people of this community. My using 'humility' is done with sincerity, a humility deepened by the splendor of the structure of this great chapel. Though we call it Gothic, it is the result of contributions of many cultures and many communities. The Rockefeller family built it, but the resources came from different communities. I, therefore, see this great edifice as Rockefeller Community Chapel. Here, all peoples, regardless of their beliefs, may come and think together. Since I view this as being characteristic of a community, then the community college connotes the same—a place where people of all beliefs and backgrounds may come, think, and work together. There is the possibility that I am in error here, for some people, even some of my colleagues, feel it is necessary for all people of the community college to think alike, look alike, act alike, and desire alike. To me, to limit students to this kind of attitude is to restrict their exposure and mobility and surely their quest for self-awareness which can best be determined after involvement with many people and experiences."

With an opening of this sort nobody can accuse you later of not having laid it on the line.

Opening Ceremonies

There are all kinds of openings, from banks to supermarkets to sports stadiums; but the principle of the opening speech is the same —pleasure and optimism. The bank may fail, the supermarket may fold, and the home team may never get out of last place; but not a hint of such catastrophes can be allowed to enter the opening-day ceremony.

The event at which you officiate may not be as vital as the opening of a Phi Beta Kappa chapter, but it will be of equal significance to the participants. So you might take a few pointers from the late Ralph J. Bunche's words at Howard University on such an occasion. After reminiscing about his own days as a professor at Howard, he continued:

"My opportunities in recent years to return to the 'Hill' have been far fewer than I might wish. But few occasions could be more auspicious or significant than the one which brings us here tonight. I am delighted to be present.

"The installation of Gamma Chapter of Phi Beta Kappa is a historic event in the annals of Howard University. It constitutes a highly significant recognition of the university community. It is a well-deserved tribute to faculty and students alike. The university is to be congratulated, and I know that a special word of commendation is due to my good friend and former colleague, Alain Locke. For I recall that many years ago Alain Locke had the dream of a Phi Beta Kappa chapter at Howard and set to work to convert dream into reality. Tonight we participate in that reality. And I am glad that this has taken place in a university in which academic freedom has real meaning."

You will note the sincere and congratulatory way in which Mr. Bunche expressed himself and his evident pleasure at being present. There could be no better guarantee for a receptive audience to the balance of his message.

Receipt of an Award

Dr. Frank Stanton, of the Columbia Broadcasting System, made a typically gracious speech on receipt of an award from the New York Advertising Council, which could serve as a model of modesty and generosity to anyone else making a similar response:

"I am deeply honored by this tribute tonight. I would like to linger over those generous words of Tex Cook, but I hesitate to indulge in any 'instant analysis.' However, I will try—on advice from high quarters—to respond 'in a very dignified and courageous way.'

"I would like to think that this award is inspired less by anything that I have done than by the contribution that broadcasting has made to a more concerned and a more informed society. And since we meet tonight under the auspices of the Advertising Council, let me note that whatever success we have achieved in this is owed in considerable measure to advertising. For—as the free press, printed and electronic, has provided advertising with an attentive forum—

advertising has furnished much of the economic sinews that have made that effort possible and has, in fact, made the free press in our time a viable reality."

Roastings

The Friars Club and other organizations hold dinners at which the principal guests make speeches hauling the guest of honor and one another over the coals. This is done in a spirit of fun, although the remarks may sound pretty rough to an outsider.

At a Hollywood Friars Club roast of Sammy Davis, Jr., Carroll (Archie Bunker) O'Connor presided over the insult merriment. When Davis got up to make his response, he referred to O'Connor, of *All in the Family*, as "the man who took bigotry, intolerance, and hatred and turned them into the fun thing they were always intended to be."

On a different occasion Bob Short, the baseball-club owner who removed his team from Washington to Texas, returned to address the National Press Club afterward. Sam Fogg, chairman of the board of the Press Club, decided to roast Short for his unpopular move.

"If you think long enough," said Mr. Fogg in his introduction, "you can think of something nice to say about Bob Short. We'll have Jack the Ripper as a speaker here later."

That kind of talk, though very funny, is also very satirical, and you must know your speaker, your guests, and your audience very well to get away with it. When you do, it can be a real gas.

Chapter 4

SUMMING
IT ALL UP

Toward the end of an address on drug abuse before the Florida Bar Association, then Attorney General John Mitchell said, "I see that I have gone on too long already." It is a wise speaker who knows when to stop and what to say when he reaches that moment. Mr. Mitchell then summarized his message in three paragraphs and a final admonishing sentence: "I urge you to begin now."

This is an example of the perfect conclusion—brief, forceful, and to the point. He knew what he wanted to say, and he said it. So should you. Keep yourself aware of the passage of time, so that you don't go on too long, and be prepared with the final words you want to impress on your audience's mind.

Inspiration

So many speeches today deal with difficult problems, from pot to pollution; but you don't want to send your listeners away too depressed to take action. Scare them if you must, but give them hope, too, and inspiration. Justice William Douglas, at the conclusion of an address to a Sierra Club conference, did just that:

"We stand on the new frontier where science and its machines threaten man. Our industrial plants and our modern conveniences have ruined many of our rivers and lakes. The roar of motors penetrates deeper and deeper into the remaining wilderness areas. Man has a constantly diminishing chance to find any retreat. Yet with the expanding population we need expanding wilderness areas where youngsters and old folks alike can escape the dreariness of life for an hour, a day, or a month and once more become in tune with the universe.

"Man was designed neither to be a *cog* in a machine as the communists conceive him, a *statistic* as science conceives him, nor a *consumer* as Madison Avenue views him.

"Man's pursuit of happiness, which Jefferson made the concern of government in our Declaration of Independence, must be our concern. While man needs a full rice bowl, he also needs more. His chief destiny is not to satisfy his physical needs. Man is a spiritual being. By our Bill of Rights we have placed many of his civil rights beyond the reach of government. We need to expand our conception of man's liberty, enlarge his individual rights, and give them priority over science.

"Those human rights include the right to put one's face in clear, pure water, to discover the wonders of sphagnum moss, and to hear the song of whippoorwills at dawn in a forest where the wilderness bowl is unbroken."

The Summary

A closing that condenses the meat of the talk in a few well-chosen sentences will send the listeners home with a memory of exactly what the speech was all about, instead of just a hazy recollection. Professor David Epel, of the Hopkins Marine Station, first gave the California Commonwealth Club a detailed description of how DDT and other chemicals were destroying life in and around the oceans; then he summarized:

"In summary, I have pointed out the danger of chemical pollution in the oceans, and I have indicated that no one is watching the world. We now have ample warning that if left unchecked, the death of the oceans will result. Coal miners used to take canaries down into the mines with them to warn about carbon monoxide poisoning. When the canaries keeled over, they knew they were in trouble and better leave fast. The oceans have also shown us their canaries. These are the pelicans not reproducing because of DDT and North Sea birds dying because of PCBs. Can we afford to wait for greater irreversible tragedies?"

You will note also how Mr. Epel goes from easily forgotten generalities to specific instances The human mind always grasps specifics better than generalities.

Solutions

If you can propose solutions for the situation you have been discussing and state them concisely, you will clarify the subject even further. Professor Epel followed his summary with a few brief proposals:

"As an immediate solution we need first the immediate establishment of an international environmental F.D.A. to prevent the release of long-lived chemicals into the environment; second, we require treaties and agencies to regulate the types of cargoes which sail the seas; finally, as both an immediate and a long-term solution, we need more basic and applied research leading to alternatives to our contaminating technology."

Call to Action

The good professor offered solutions which his listeners could not at once, and by themselves, bring about. You can have an even stronger ending if your audience is in a position to correct the problems you have been discussing. When Samuel C. Jackson, assistant secretary of the Department of Housing, addressed a section of the American Bar Association, he discussed metropolitan housing problems and their legal ramifications. Then he put it to the lawyers that their anticity bias might eventually cause cities to become obsolete. Said Mr. Jackson:

"This question of attitudes is especially important for the legal profession to realize, for lawyers more than most people have the ability to shape things according to how they perceive them. The legal profession thus has an enormous responsibility for what our cities are and will become." Note how he places the responsibility. Then he encourages them to use their influence:

"All of you, whether you teach, research, practice, or serve in public capacities, have great talent, great influence, and an unrivaled opportunity to play a role in shaping the future of American cities. I hope that in some small way I have encouraged many of you to deepen your commitment to thus serve."

Finally he gave them that forceful conclusion that always ends a speech on an upbeat. Mr. Jackson used a powerful quote from Dr. W. E. B. Du Bois: "If we are told that it is impossible—then it shall become the *impossible must*."

The Appropriate Quote

A quote from someone who was more of a master of words than yourself can often give your speech that necessary final punch. Dr.

A. J. Haagen-Smit, of the California Institute of Technology, for example, concluded an Earth Day speech with a quote from R. S. Scorer,* which summed up the meaning of his entire talk:

> We know what does the damage and we know what is not good.
> But nothing's done, because it's not completely understood.
> We have the know-how and the wealth, but do nothing until
> Our view of life provides us also with determined will.
> We are fallible, of course, but must we always gasp for breath
> Until we fully understand the chemistry of death.

When the United States Undersecretary of State wanted to end a commencement speech on the generation gap, he wound up with an appropriate quote from Carl Sandburg:†

> Man is a long time coming.
> Man will yet win.
> Brother may yet line up with brother.

Martin Luther King, Jr., was particularly fond of a quote from a Southern preacher:

> Lord, we ain't what we ought to be,
> We ain't what we want to be,
> We ain't what we're going to be,
> But, thank the Lord, we ain't what we was.

The Human-Interest Story

After a talk full of declamations and statistics it warms people up and gives your material life if you can illustrate it with a human-interest story. Donald Greve, of Sequoyah Industries, tried this in an address on job opportunities for the American Indian, when he concluded with the story of a small Indian boy who was attending the opening ceremony for a carpet factory. In his excitement he pushed his way under the ropes and past the important officials to point to

---

*Quotation from R. S. Scorer reprinted with permission of the author.

†Permission to quote from *The People, Yes* by Carl Sandburg granted by Harcourt Brace Jovanovich.

his father, standing by the drying oven, ready to do his job, and proudly declared, "That's my daddy!"

The story can be followed up with a tie-in to the theme of the speech, which in Mr. Greve's case was a request for "not a handout, but a hand up, to your fellow Americans—the American Indian."

The One-Liner

It has been said by authorities on after-dinner speaking that the successful ingredients are the quotation, the joke, and the platitude. The platitude is, of course, an overworked saying like "Might makes right," "The love of money is the root of all evil," or "Don't put all your eggs in one basket."

You can give a lift to the closing of a speech with the twist on the platitude, known as the one-liner. For instance, here's a twist on "Practice what you preach": "Some folks practice what they preach; others just practice preaching."

On "Truth is beauty": "If truth is beauty and beauty is truth, how come all pretty girls lie about their age?"

On "Appearances are deceiving": "Appearances are deceiving—a dollar looks the same as it did ten years ago."

On "There are two sides to every argument": "Isn't it strange how easily we can understand the two sides of any argument when it doesn't concern us?"

On "Destiny shapes our ends": "Destiny shapes our ends, but calories shape our middles."

On "You can fool some of the people all of the time": "You can fool some of the people all of the time . . . and chances are if you're not careful, you'll be one of them."

Wrapping It Up

As you approach the close of your speech, try to hold your listener's interest while at the same time letting him know he'll soon be off the hook. A paragraph that almost anyone could adapt for his own purposes was used by Howard Frazier, of the Consumer Federation: "There is a saying that the 'tall timber catches the wind.' This audience is definitely tall timber, and tonight I'm afraid I've been the wind and it is high time I quit blowing."

In a talk on freedom of the press Helen Delich Bentley began her penultimate paragraph with a phrase very useful to the public speaker:

"Let me leave you with this one, final thought—would we be here tonight and would I be speaking with such freedom if you were bloc-nation journalists meeting in Moscow and I were the Minister of Merchant Marine and your term of address for me was commissar?

"Happy 'freedom of the press,' comrades!"

Winding It Down

Some speeches seem written by the time clock. The speaker keeps going until his allotted time is up, then says, "Thank you," and sits down so you'll know it's over. The true orator ends with an unmistakable verbal flourish that signals the end, like American Legion Commander J. Milton Patrick:

"These are *united* States. We *are* a resolute people. Our *trust* is in God and Country.

"An America that is united and determined and true to its spiritual and patriotic heritage will not be found wanting—in the present crisis or in any to come."

Mr. Patrick didn't have to pick up his notes and return to his seat to telegraph the end of that speech.

Fred C. Foy, of the Koppers Company, ended a talk on technology with the same kind of positive, conclusive statement:

"No, my grandsons, even you agree it's too late to abandon technology. Machines and technology and medicine have done too much for man to be rejected for the problems they have brought with them.

"Any fool can turn his back on a problem. It is the men who solve the insoluble who are the hope of mankind."

Chapter 5

SOMETHING
TO REMEMBER

The conclusion of a speech can be like the little souvenir taken home from a banquet—perfume, a pin, a pen, a pencil, or a cigarette lighter. It is casually picked up, and sometime later the guest comes across it to be reminded pleasantly of the occasion. Your closing words should also give the listener something to remember you by when he gets home.

Dramatize

When Helen Hayes was honored with a citation from the Salvation Army for her charitable work, she closed her acceptance speech with an appropriate tribute to the organization's endeavors, a recitation from Shakespeare's *The Merchant of Venice.*

> The quality of mercy is not strain'd;
> It droppeth as the gentle rain from heaven
> Upon the place beneath: it is twice bless'd;
> It blesseth him that gives and him that takes.

Helen Hayes doing Shakespeare was truly something to remember.

Those of us not blessed with dramatic talent can still produce an impressive closing by not giving the audience all the best material at the start, but saving some for a sock finish, like a magician pulling a rabbit out of a hat.

Save the Best for Last

Humorist Jean Shepherd has for years been doing monologues which he delivers as though they were extemporaneous talks about subjects that just that minute occurred to him. Such a projection of informality is the result of years of professional experience on stage, television, and radio; but he has one trick you might adapt to your own use. He starts off with a remark like "Did I ever tell you about that awful, embarrassing experience I had back at Warren G. Harding High, when I played the sousaphone between the halves of the big game?" Then he'll go off on a description of the instrument and numerous other related stories, while the listener is kept in suspense as to what happened on that awful day at Warren G. Harding High. After forty minutes or so he'll get back to his opening teaser and tell the tale we've been waiting all that time to hear. The relief from suspense is so great that the listener remembers the story much more vividly than if it had been told straight. This might be called the "dropping the other shoe" technique, and it is a good one.

Keep to the Point

Mr. Shepherd's technique must be used with discretion, however. It is very easy during a speech, as you warm up to your subject, to go off on a tangent that particularly interests you and then discover you are so far out on a limb you've nearly hanged yourself. Have some notations on your reminder cards which will draw you back gracefully to the point you want your audience to take away with them. Don't leave it up to chance.

When you get into your closing words, keep the delivery direct and straightforward. Long-winded sentences are difficult to understand and impossible to remember. Like Brand X noodles, your meaning gets lost in the sauce.

Some speakers can hold an audience in their hands to the very end with high-flown words and spellbinding oratory, but when it's all over, and someone asks you, "What did he say?" you can't answer. You just don't know. Pat Paulsen gets his laughs in his monologues that start out making sense and end up in double-talk because people recognize it as the same kind of gobbledygook with which the speaker wound up his talk at the last meeting they attended.

Eddie Miller, director of the Speakers Services Department of the American Medical Association, calls this "the malady of swollen language." Some examples of it are calling a library "a study materials resource center" or a hospital "an organizational modality." This malady has turned janitors into custodians, street cleaners into sanitary engineers, and ear, nose, and throat doctors into otorhinolaryngologists. In swollen language we don't talk to anyone; we "establish a meaningful dialogue."

According to Mr. Miller, Winston Churchill's message after Dunkirk in 1940 is a fine example of keeping to the point. He said, in part: "We shall defend our island, whatever the cost may be. We shall fight on the beaches. We shall fight on the landing grounds. We shall fight in the fields and in the streets. We shall fight in the hills. We shall never surrender."

Mr. Miller suggests that a less accomplished speaker might have concluded, "We shall oppose the aggressors through the optimal mobilization and implementation of all existing defense-oriented modalities," and never have been heard of again.

Repeat for Emphasis

Sometimes the best closing is a repetition of your opening, expressed in a slightly different way. Don't strain to find new words, however. Many English purists frown on repeated use of the same words, and speakers will go crazy trying to find synonyms for words they've used before, ending up calling a baby anything from a nestling to a neonate, when what they mean is just simply *baby*; or referring to a charitable organization as everything from philanthropic to eleemosynary. And so on. Leave out the fancy variations. Just stick to a simple repetition of the thoughts you have expressed at the start, if that is what you want them to remember you by.

Itemize

A good way to clarify your closing is to list your points numerically and follow them with a couple of strong statements that lay the matter under discussion right on the line. Secretary of Labor George Shultz used this kind of a conclusion in a speech on the Family Assistance Act. He defined the act and then endorsed it as follows:

"The Family Assistance Act relies on basically three approaches.

"First, it attempts to maintain the dignity of the poor. We will stop undermining their self-respect and self-reliance.

"Second, it removes the barriers that exist to becoming employed, such as lack of training, basic education, and child care.

"Third, it provides financial incentives to seek training and employment.

"The Family Assistance Act is not cheap. It will cost the federal government an added four to four point four billion dollars in its first year of operation. But it is an investment which promises substantial savings in the future, both as a present generation is lifted economically and as the next generation is plucked from the poverty cycle."

Specific Illustration

The closing of a talk can be given added emphasis by citing a concrete example. A speaker who has been discussing the evils of water pollution, for instance, could end his speech with the story of Tom Hetzel, the marathon swimmer. Tom has swum the English Channel and many other bodies of water around the world. He would like to do marathon swimming in this country but finds it nearly impossible. What body of water could be used? Lake Erie? The Mississippi? New York Harbor? Forget it! A marathon swim around Manhattan would be a great event, he says, but by the time the contestants reached the end of the course they'd be ready for the hospital.

Subtle Flattery

There is no better way to disarm criticism than to pretend you welcome it. When John W. Macy, Jr., president of the Corporation for Public Broadcasting, addressed the National Press Club, he was talking to some of television's severest critics. After citing many of the good things that have been done in the medium, he concluded:

"I would be testing your patience—while exercising my enthusiasm—to continue this catalog. Suffice it to say that when I survey the potential of public broadcasting, I agree with E. B. White when he told the Carnegie Commission on Educational Television several years ago:

" 'I think television should be the visual counterpart of the literary essay, should arouse our dreams, satisfy our hunger for beauty, take us on journeys, enable us to participate in events, present great drama and music, explore the sea and the sky and the woods and the hills. It should be our Lyceum, our Chautauqua, our Minsky's, and our Camelot.

" 'It should restate and clarify the social dilemma and the political pickle.' "

Mr. Macy continued modestly: "We have not yet measured up to Mr. White's prescription. We are determined to do so. What's more, we are determined to fill the desperate need of the American people today to become involved in the examination and definition of the problems that beset them and the search for solutions." He concluded flatteringly, "With your help we will succeed!"

The Humorous Anecdote

A story that illustrates your theme and at the same time sends your audience away with a chuckle or two is always a good bet. This book provides many humorous stories you can tie in with your speeches. The subject of your story doesn't even need to be directly related to your talk, if you can switch it around to fit, as Tom Anderson did near the close of his D.A.R. speech:

"And we need to get to work. God alone can save the world—but God won't save the world alone, nor will prayer alone. No matter how difficult the task or how long the odds, let us never quit trying.

"Like the fellow on the golf tee who said to his companion: 'I've got to do well here! That's my mother-in-law on the clubhouse porch.'

" 'Don't be silly!' replied his friend. 'That's over two hundred yards—you'll never hit her from here!' "

If *you* were looking for a story to tell at the conclusion of a speech on the subject "A Constitutional Government under God," would you look under the heading "Golf" or "Mother-in-law"? *He* evidently did, and the results were okay. So don't be discouraged if you don't always find something suitable under your main subject. Use your imagination, and give it free rein.

Ladies and gentlemen, I thank you!

Part II

The Toastmaster General's Favorite Jokes

ABSTINENCE

"Did you hear about poor old Charlie?" asked one golfer of another.

"No, what happened?"

"Well, you know he got married. First his wife made him cut out drinking. Then she made him cut out smoking. Then she made him cut out going out with the guys to play cards and golf."

"That's terrible," said the second golfer, "but what happened to Charlie?"

"Now he's cutting out paper dolls."

A prosperous man was accosted by a disreputable-looking bum who asked for some money for a meal.

"Have a cigarette."

"Thanks, but I don't smoke," replied the bum.

"Then come inside with me and let me buy you a drink."

"No, I don't drink."

"Then let me give you this lottery ticket."

"No, I never gamble. Couldn't you spare some money for a decent meal?"

"I can do better than that. You come home with me. I'll cook you the biggest steak you ever saw."

"That's very kind of you, but wouldn't it be easier if you just gave me the money?"

"Easier, yes, but I want my wife to see what happens to a man who doesn't drink, smoke, or gamble."

A loving young couple were taking a romantic canoe ride out on the lake when suddenly a squall hit. The young man was terrified by the intensity of the wind and rain—so terrified that he began to pray, "O Lord, save us, and I'll give up smoking. I'll give up drinking. I'll give up gambling. I'll even give up——"

Just then his companion cried, "Hold it, Reggie, don't give up anything else—I think the storm is breaking."

ACCIDENTS

A very pretty girl smashed head-on into a car coming up the street. She got out of her car and rushed to the driver of the other car. He was furious until he got a good look at her.

"I'm terribly sorry," she said, sobbing. "It was all my fault."

"Nonsense," he replied comfortingly. "The fault was entirely mine. I saw you coming from at least three blocks away. I had plenty of time to get out of your way."

ACCOUNTANTS

They say some guys fear their accountants more than Judgment Day. I know one who must. One day he had his secretary send for his accountant. When the man appeared in his office, he bellowed, "Listen, you, I won't put up with much more of this. Last year I caught you forging checks with my name. This year I know you embezzled at least five thousand out of my business. Last week I found out that you tried to sell my biggest competitor some of my business secrets, and if that isn't enough, I even caught you making advances to my youngest daughter. Now I'm warning you for the last time: The next little thing I catch you doing—out you go!"

ACTORS

A troupe of down-and-out actors was touring Africa. On their way from one engagement to the next they were attacked and captured by a band of cannibals. The entire troupe was herded back to the cannibals' village, and from the hungry look in their captors' eyes, the actors knew the end was near—all, that is, but the leading man, who indignantly demanded to speak to the chief. The chief granted him a few minutes, and the actor, thinking to impress the "ignorant savage," informed him that he was a famous Shakespearean actor and much too well known to end his career as a snack. To emphasize the point the actor launched into Hamlet's famous "To be or not to be. . . ." The chief endured these histrionics for a few minutes and then motioned for his favorite wife. She came obediently to his side, and he whispered a few words in her ear. She stepped back, eyed the actor up and down, thought for a minute, and was heard to say, "I think we might even have enough left over for ham sandwiches."

—●—

Two old troupers were reminiscing.

"I remember the time I played Hamlet," said the first. "When I did the death scene, the audience broke down and cried."

"What's so great about that?" sniffed the second.

"When I did that death scene, my insurance agent was in the audience, and he left the theater to pay my wife my life insurance."

—●—

A broken-down Shakespearean actor was offered a role in a movie. When he learned that his role consisted of exactly three lines, he was outraged.

"I refuse to do it! The very idea is an insult! It would destroy my reputation."

"I know," replied his agent. "Figure it's your one big chance."

—●—

"You know, at my last performance I had the audience glued to their seats," boasted an actor whose talent was far exceeded by his conceit.

"Really?" replied his latest costar. "How very clever of you to think of it."

—●—

Two actors were talking about a comedian who was notorious for his off-color jokes.

"The thing that really gets me about that guy," said the first actor, "is the way he always says he's never told a joke he wouldn't tell his own mother."

"It's true," said the second, "but then you must realize, old boy, his mother was a stripper."

—●—

Why is a termite like a frustrated actor?
Because he keeps trying to bring the house down.

ADAM

Young Maryjane said, "You know, Mom, Jack says he was at that costume ball last week, but I couldn't tell him from Adam."

"Good grief," exclaimed her mother. "You mean he dressed like *that*?"

ADVERTISING

Miss Lewis stepped out of her classroom for a moment, and when she returned, someone had scrawled "I am the best kisser in the whole world" on the blackboard.

"Who wrote that?" asked the teacher.

"I did," confessed Jimmy Brown.

"You will stay after school today."

"See, it doesn't pay to be such a smart aleck," hissed one of his classmates.

"Maybe not," replied young Jim, "but it sure pays to advertise."

—●—

Malcolm G. Krebbs was the last of the old diehards who believed in doing business without advertising, and like so many others he found that his philosophy just didn't work anymore. So he finally went to an advertising agency, but with great misgivings. Mr. Krebbs just couldn't manage to understand the principle behind advertising until his account executive explained it to him like this: Doing business without advertising is like winking at a girl in the dark; you know what you are doing, but nobody else does.

—●—

A teen-ager I know answered one of those lurid ads for a book that promised it would tell "everything a young girl should know to prepare her for one of the most important aspects of marriage—complete with detailed instructions and illustrations." After several weeks of anticipation the mailman delivered a book that fulfilled every promise: a cookbook.

—●—

A minister who believed firmly in advertising had a sign erected in front of his church which proclaimed, "IF YOU ARE TIRED OF SIN, COME IN." Some enterprising member of his congregation who also believed in advertising, however, scrawled the additional message, "IF YOU'RE NOT, CALL GRANDVIEW 9-6001."

—●—

It was the shoplifter's ninth offense at the same department store. The store president had the crook brought to his office.

"If you don't mind my asking," said the president, "why is it always my store you pick to rob?"

"Simple," replied the thief. "You always advertise such terrific bargains."

—●—

Advertising is just a picture of a beautiful girl eating, holding, driving, wearing, or standing in front of something nobody really needs but somebody wants to sell.

—●—

Mary was sitting alone on the couch when her mother came in and turned on the light.

"Why, what's the matter, dear?" asked her mother. "Why are you sitting here in the dark? Did you and John have a fight?"

"Oh, no, nothing like that," replied Mary. "As a matter of fact, John asked me to marry him."

"Well, then, why do you look so sad?"

"Oh, mother, it's just that I don't know if I could marry an advertising executive."

"But what's wrong with marrying a man who is in advertising?"

"Well, how would you feel if a man who was proposing to you told you that it was a once-in-a-lifetime, never-to-be-repeated, special offer?"

AFFAIRS

Two very successful Jewish restaurateurs were playing golf one afternoon. The first man teed off and stepped aside for his friend. The second man seemed terribly disconcerted. He stumbled up to the tee, but his hands shook so much he couldn't even set up the ball.

His friend watched in amazement as his nervous companion finally got himself set up, only to take a swing at the ball and miss it altogether.

"Harry," said Jake, "a Sam Snead you never were, but this is ridiculous. Is maybe something on your mind? Perhaps something is upsetting you that maybe we can discuss?"

Harry looked sadly at his friend and said, "Jake, what can I say? I've just discovered something so terrible I can't even tell you."

"Don't be silly. I'm your best friend. Nothing is so bad you can't tell me."

"Maybe you're right," said Harry. "Maybe I'll feel better if I tell you. I just found out that my married daughter is having an affair."

"You don't say," said Jake. "So who's catering it?"

—•—

A hotel just outside of town was having great difficulty getting conventions and weddings and other lucrative business. So the enterprising young manager decided to advertise. He took several ads in the local papers, but his pièce de résistance was a huge neon sign he had placed right out in front of the hotel. Needless to say, there were many amused passersby, for the sign pleaded, "HAVE YOUR NEXT AFFAIR HERE."

AGE

"How's your daughter?" asked one father of another.

"Well," replied the hip parent, "she's at that awkward age. She's too old to be a Bluebird and too young to be a Bunny."

—•—

A man is getting old when the only gleam in his eye comes from the reflection of light through his bifocals.

—•—

Mr. Bennett was an elderly gentleman who had been asked too often if old age had its advantages. He finally came up with a reply guaranteed to squelch the pest who asked. "It sure does, sonny," he would say. "Now I can sing while I brush my teeth."

—•—

Mr. Jones found himself in need of a secretary, so he called the local employment agency.

"I don't care how she looks," he said to the woman on the phone, "just as long as she can type and take dictation."

"Certainly, sir," came the cool reply, "but we like to see to it that our girls have steady employment. Perhaps you might be better off with temporary office help."

"I don't want 'temporary' help," he replied. "What ever gave you that idea?"

"Nothing, sir," she replied sweetly. "It's just that a man who doesn't care how his secretary looks is usually about ready to retire."

—●—

"You know," confided one wife to her best friend, "I just don't know what to do about Charlie. He's at that dangerous age."

"What do you mean?"

"Oh, you know. He's trying to prove that he's just as good as he *never* was."

—●—

Mr. and Mrs. Potts were being visited by some reporters on the occasion of Mr. Potts's ninety-ninth birthday. One of the reporters shook Mr. Potts's hand and told him it was wonderful that a man could live to such an age. Mrs. Potts had other thoughts on the subject.

"Just listen to that young fool," she said to another reporter who happened to be at her side. "Now, what's so wonderful about being ninety-nine? He never did nothing worthwhile in his whole life except get old, and it took him a hell of a long time to do that."

—●—

While reviewing a census form, a clerk noticed that one man had entered the figures "110" and "115" in the spaces marked "Age of mother if living" and "Age of father if living." Thinking this to be most unusual, he called the home of the man who had filled out the form.

"Are your parents really that old?" asked the clerk.

"No" was the reply. "But they would be *if* they were living."

ALLIGATORS

A man and his Indian guide were camping in the Everglades. In the middle of the night the man woke up yelling that an alligator had bitten off his foot.

"Which one?" asked his guide.

"How should I know?" the man moaned. "They all look alike to me."

—•—

While touring the United States, an Englishman spent a few weeks in the South. He decided to take a steamboat ride on the Mississippi. He was fascinated by the alligators he saw near the banks.

"Is the alligator an amphibious animal?" he inquired of one of the mates.

"Amphibious, hell!" snapped the old salt. "That critter would bite your foot off if you gave him half a chance."

AMNESIA

Do you know the difference between amnesia and magnesia? Simple, the person with amnesia doesn't know where he's going.

ANCESTRY

A pretentious bore bragged, "My ancestors came over on the *Mayflower*."

"How fortunate for you," replied an elegant lady standing nearby. "The immigration laws are *much* stricter these days."

ANIMALS

A zoo-keeper was headed for the kangaroo cage right around feeding time when, much to his surprise, the kangaroo jumped right over the ten-foot fence and went hopping out of sight. The startled zoo-keeper dashed up to the cage and confronted a woman who was standing in front of it.

"What happened?" he asked.

"I haven't the faintest notion," she replied. "All I did was tickle him a little."

"Well, lady," he replied, "I guess you'd better tickle me in the same place. I'm the one who has to catch him."

—●—

A lion was stalking through the jungle one day when he came across a bull. The lion and the bull got into a tremendous battle, but in the end the lion killed the bull and ate him up. The lion was so pleased with himself that he threw back his head and roared and roared. The noise attracted a hunter who followed the sound until he found the lion. The hunter took aim and killed the lion with a single shot.

The moral of the story: When you are full of bull, it is wise to keep your mouth shut.

ANTIQUES

Mr. Barnaby, owner of a priceless collection of antique Roman urns, was gracious enough to permit a local museum to exhibit his treasures. The movers arrived early one morning and began packing the urns while Barnaby hovered over them nervously.

"Do be careful with that urn," he cautioned one burly mover. "It's nearly three thousand years old."

"Don't worry about a thing, Mac," replied the mover. "I'll treat it like it was brand-new."

ART

A proud father was showing off some of his daughter's artwork to a friend.

"This is one of her landscapes," the father informed his friend. "She painted it abroad."

"Well," replied the friend, "that explains it. I never saw a landscape that looked like that in this country."

—●—

A middle-aged lady was strolling through a gallery of very modern art. She stopped in front of a rather violent painting full of huge splotches of the most unpleasant colors imaginable. Noticing her disapproval, the young man who had painted the picture stepped forward and demanded to know what she thought of the painting. The lady admitted that she didn't care very much for it. The young man then informed her that he was the artist.

"Tell me," she asked, "why do you paint like that?"

"I paint," he replied, "the way I feel."

"Oh," she replied sympathetically, "have you tried bicarbonate of soda?"

—●—

Mr. Robbespierre Van Drake, the world's most famous modern artist, was granting an interview on his sixtieth birthday.

"Mr. Van Drake," said one reporter, "can you remember what it was that inspired you to begin painting in your now famous 'futuristic' style?"

"I certainly can remember," replied the great man. "My model had the hiccups."

ATHEISM

Overheard between two tropical fish: "Okay, wise guy, if there is no God, just answer me one question: Who changes the water every day?"

ATTENTIVENESS

Definition of a good listener: A man who can listen to a joke without having it remind him of one of his own.

AUTHORITY

"Young man," said the dignified matron in one of the most exclusive shops in town, "I would like to speak to someone with a little authority around here."

"Well, ma'am," replied the clerk, "I guess you want to talk to me. I have as little authority as anyone in this whole store."

AZTECS

One not so ancient Aztec had quite a line. He was overheard telling one of his latest conquests, "Look at it this way, baby. The next time the chief decides it's time to sacrifice another virgin, you won't have a thing to worry about."

BABIES

Eight-year-old Amy came charging in from the backyard, where she and three little boys had been playing.

"Mommy, Mommy," she called breathlessly, "can I have babies?"

"No, darling," replied her mother, "not for several more years yet."

"Okay, boys," shouted little Amy as she charged back out into the yard, "same game."

—●—

A precocious seven-year-old asked her mother for a baby brother.

Her mother was taken aback by the request but said in a soothing tone, "I'm afraid that just isn't possible, darling. Babies cost a great deal of money, and Daddy and I just can't afford one right now."

"Mommy," said her daughter in a most exasperated tone, "women don't *buy* babies. I think you and I should have a little talk!"

BANKRUPTCY

"Do you think his bankruptcy was due to a lack of brains?"

"Only partly. Actually it was due to a lack and a lass."

BARBERS

A man went into a barbershop and decided to have a manicure while the barber shaved him.

"How about going out tonight, baby?"

"I'm sorry, but I couldn't," replied the manicurist. "You see, I'm married."

"Don't worry about it. Just phone your husband and tell him you have to work late tonight."

"Why don't you tell him yourself?" asked the manicurist. "After all, he's shaving you."

BARGAINS

I know a girl who just loves bargains. She'll buy the biggest size every time—claims it saves her money. Her sister was the same way before the accident. It was a terrible thing. She bought one of those giant, economy-size cans of hair spray, but the first time she used it, she pressed the button and damn near blew her head off.

BARTENDERS

Bartenders see a great many different kinds of people, and every single bartender has a favorite story about a guy who came into his bar. This one concerns the bartender at a very posh gentlemen's club in New York who was on duty when a distinguished gentleman seated himself at the bar but made no attempt to order a drink. The bartender inquired what the gentleman would have, but the man replied that he was not drinking because he had tried liquor once and hadn't liked it. The bartender hated to see the man just sitting there, so he tried offering him a cigar.

"No, thank you," was his firm reply. "I tried a cigar once, but I didn't like it."

The bartender persisted in trying to make the customer comfortable, so he suggested that perhaps if he stepped into the billiard room, he might find a friendly game of cards to sit in on.

"Oh, no," he replied. "I did gamble once—didn't care for it at all. I'll just sit here, if you don't mind. You see, I'm waiting for my son."

"Oh," replied the bartender sympathetically, "your only child, I assume."

—•—

A man went into a bar for a quick drink. When he had finished his drink, the bartender presented him with a live lobster.

"Thanks, I love lobster," said the customer. "I'll take him home for dinner."

"He's already had his dinner," said the bartender. "Why don't you take him to a movie?"

—•—

"Daddy," said little Bill, "what do you call a man who helps you contact the spirit world?"

"A bartender, my boy."

—•—

I have a friend who used to be a used-car salesman. He finally decided to get out of the business, so he bought himself a little bar and grill. It's the only joint in town where you can trade in your olives on a new martini.

—●—

"There must be some mistake!" exclaimed the honest patron after examining his bar bill. "I had three scotch and waters, and this bill comes to only fifteen cents."

"No mistake, pal," replied the bartender. "I charged you only a nickel a drink."

"That's amazing," replied the customer, "but how can you afford to run a place like this if you charge only a nickel a drink? Aren't you afraid you'll wind up out of business?"

"No," replied the bartender, "but, then, I'm not the owner."

"Oh," replied the customer, "where is the owner?"

"Upstairs," replied the bartender, "with my wife. And what he's doing to her up there I'm doing to him down here!"

BASEBALL

A man decided to take his wife to a baseball game, but because of her dillydallying they didn't arrive at the park until the sixth inning. Naturally, the husband was furious.

He turned to the man in the next seat and said, "Say, pal, what's the score?"

"Nothing to nothing."

"There," said his wife, "you see? You were in such a hurry, and we haven't missed a thing."

—●—

A man went to a psychiatrist and complained that baseball had become an obsession.

"Doc, you just have to help me," he said, moaning. "It's so bad that I can't sleep. I no sooner close my eyes than I'm out there on the pitcher's mound or running around the bases. I wake up more exhausted than when I went to bed. What can I do?"

"Well," replied the doctor, "you must make a conscious effort not to dream about baseball. When you close your eyes, you must try to imagine that you are lying there with a beautiful girl in your arms."

"Are you crazy, Doc?" shouted the patient. "I'll miss my turn at bat."

BIBLE

A traveling preacher was trapped by a snowstorm at one of the farms on his circuit. The lady of the house was delighted to have such a distinguished guest and did everything she could think of to make him comfortable. When evening fell, she inquired if the preacher would like to read the Bible and pray before retiring. He assured his hostess that he would be grateful for the privilege, so she turned to her young son Abner and said, "Go into the parlor, dear, and bring me that big book Mama and Papa are always reading." The boy disappeared for a moment and then returned triumphantly carrying the Sears, Roebuck catalog.

—•—

A little old lady was mailing her grandson a package for his birthday. One of the things it contained was a Bible.

The postal clerk inspected the package and asked, "Does it contain anything breakable?"

"Oh," replied the little old lady dryly, "only the Ten Commandments."

—•—

"All right, ladies and gentlemen, who will open the bidding on this magnificent bust of Aristotle?" asked the auctioneer.

"Young man," said one of the well-dressed matrons among the bidders, "that is a bust of Plato, not Aristotle."

"If you say so, ma'am," the auctioneer agreed. "I never could keep those guys in the Bible straight."

—•—

"Why do you read the Bible so much?" asked little Johnny.

"Well, sonny," replied his old grandmother, "I guess you might say I'm cramming for my final exams."

BIRTH CONTROL

A sweet young thing went to see her doctor because she was afraid she was pregnant. He assured her that she wasn't and offered her her choice of several different types of birth-control measures; however, she refused them all for one reason or another.

"Isn't there anything else you can suggest?" she pleaded.

"Just one thing," replied the doctor. "Drink lots of milk."

"Before or after?" she inquired.

"Instead of," he replied firmly.

BOARDERS

An irate boarder threatened to sue his landlady for misrepresenting the facts. "I am well aware, madam, that you advertised that this room included 'bed and board.' What I did not know then was that they are one and the same."

—●—

Two women were discussing their apartments in New York. One complained bitterly about the rent she paid for her apartment, which she assured her friend "would fit into the living room of the house I was raised in." Her friend was sympathetic but admitted that she really couldn't complain.

"But," protested her friend, "your apartment is even smaller than mine. Doesn't it bother you?"

"Not really," admitted her friend. "You see," she said, "my mother raised eleven of us in a four-room shack."

"How on earth did she ever manage?" exclaimed her friend.

"It was tough," admitted her friend, "but we took in boarders."

BORES

An unlucky dignitary was cornered by a very talkative woman at a Washington cocktail party. She rambled at great length while the poor man nursed his drink and looked around for someone to rescue him.

Finally she paused for breath and then, as an afterthought, said, "Why, you haven't said anything for the last half hour."

"Well," came the exasperated reply, "that makes it unanimous."

BOSTON

A grande dame from Boston and a New York society matron found themselves seated opposite each other at a fashionable dinner party. They took an immediate dislike to one another and soon managed to monopolize the conversation with a rather heated discussion of the merits of their own social status.

"You know," said the first lady in icy tones, "we in Boston place all our emphasis on good breeding."

"Well," replied the New Yorker, "I can certainly understand why, but we in New York try to find time to develop other interests."

BRAINS

Those who still believe that the race is to the swift even after hearing the story of the tortoise and the hare might consider this story. A rather portly gentleman was having a drink in his favorite tavern when a tall, athletic-looking young man stood up and demanded to know if there was any man in the place who would be willing to race with him. There were no takers, but the young man persisted.

"I'll give you any odds you like," he boasted. "I'll even give you a head start." But still there were no takers. "I'll even let you choose the course," he bragged.

"I'll accept your challenge," said the portly little man as he proceeded to finish his drink.

The young man looked at him scornfully. "Why, you haven't a chance," he scoffed.

"If you meant what you said about giving me a head start and letting me select the course, I am willing to bet you one hundred dollars that I will win," insisted the man as he started in on his second drink.

"If you insist," said the young man, "but it seems a crime to take your money. What course do you choose?"

"Well," said his clever opponent, "I thought I'd race you up a stepladder."

THE BRITISH

An English gentleman took a cab in New York City, and during the ride the cabdriver asked him to solve a riddle.

"I'm thinking of a person who has the same father and the same mother as me, but this person is not my sister and not my brother. Who is this person?"

The Englishman thought and thought, but he just couldn't solve the riddle. "I give up," he cried.

"It's simple, Mac," said the driver. "The person is me."

"By jove!" exclaimed the Englishman. "That is a good one. I must remember that."

A few weeks later this very same Englishman, back home in London, posed this riddle to some members of his club. "I am thinking of a person who has the same mother and the same father as me, but this person is not my sister and not my brother. Who is this person?"

His friends thought and thought, but none could solve the riddle. "We give up, old boy," they said. "Tell us, who is this person?"

The Englishman practically crowed in triumph. "It's a taxi driver in New York City!"

—●—

A drunken cowboy charged into a saloon on the old frontier, brandishing his Colt .45 and yelling, "All right, you mangy varmints, clear out and give a man some elbow room." All the customers fled except for one British gentleman who was seated at a table in the far corner. The cowboy sauntered over to the table and said, "Maybe you didn't hear me, partner. I said for all the mangy varmints to clear out."

"I heard you, old boy," replied the British gentleman, "and I must say, there certainly were a lot of them, weren't there?"

—●—

A tourist and his wife were strolling over the castle grounds one lovely autumn day when a bullet whizzed past the lady's ear. The man was outraged and went crashing through the woods after the careless hunter. He came upon the earl, who was preparing to have another shot.

"Hey," shouted the tourist, "you nearly shot my wife!"

"Terribly sorry, old boy," replied the penitent nobleman. "Have a shot at mine. She's right over there."

—●—

An American socialite atended a garden party at a stately country home in England.

"You American girls haven't got half the complexions we English women have," said one English guest cattily. "I can't imagine what our English men find so attractive about your pasty-white faces."

"Oh," replied the American demurely, "it isn't our white faces that attract your English men; it's our green backs."

—●—

Three deaf British gentlemen were traveling on a train bound for London.

The first said, "Pardon me, conductor, what station is this?"

"Wembley, sir," answered the conductor.

"Good Lord!" exclaimed the second Englishman. "I am sure it's Thursday."

"So am I," agreed the third. "Let's all go into the bar car and have a drink."

—•—

The master had reason to believe that Mrs. Pringle, the new British housekeeper, had been nipping at his liquor supply. When he confronted her with this suspicion, however, she was outraged.

"I'll have you know," she declared firmly, "I come from honest English stock."

"That may be," replied her employer, "but it isn't your parents I'm interested in. What concerns me is your *Scotch* extraction."

—•—

Two old Englishmen were having lunch at their club.

"I tell you, old fellow, it was terrible," said the first. "My canoe tipped over in the middle of the lake, and I thought my time was up. My whole life flashed before me in a series of crystal-clear pictures."

"You don't say," replied his friend. "I don't suppose one of those pictures was of me lending you fifty pounds last month at Ascot."

—•—

Two English gentlemen were lunching at their club. The conversation got around to old friends, and one said, "I say, old boy, what ever became of old Chauncey? Last I heard, he was safariing in Africa, but that was years ago."

"Still there," replied his companion. "Shocking thing is, they say he's taken to living with a gorilla."

"You don't say," said the first. "Male or female?"

"Female, of course! Nothing queer about old Chauncey."

—•—

Overheard at Ascot:

"I say, old chap, hear you buried your wife last month."

"Had to. Dead, you know."

BROKERS

Trying to impress a prospective client with his business acumen, a would-be tycoon snapped on his intercom and said gruffly, "Miss Holister, call my broker immediately."

"Certainly, sir," replied his secretary. "Stock or pawn?"

BROTHERS-IN-LAW

My wife's brother is a deep thinker—or at least that's what he'd like everyone to think. He delves into the mysteries of life. He's spent years trying to figure out *why* Bill Bailey won't go home.

BROTHER'S KEEPERS

Just recently an ape escaped from our local zoo. Several hours later the beast was finally found in the reading room of the town library. He was poring over the first chapter of Genesis, and he also had a copy of Darwin's *Origin of the Species*. When a policeman asked the ape what he was doing, the ape replied, "I'm trying to figure out once and for all if I am my brother's keeper, or if I'm my keeper's brother."

BUREAUCRATS

Two Americans were going through customs after returning from France. The customs officials were being particularly thorough, and one of the Americans was growing increasingly annoyed at having his belongings rifled. Finally, unable to contain his annoyance, he began a tirade against the official. Undaunted by the outburst, the official kept right on searching, all the while being told that there was nothing in the suitcases but clothes. Finally, in the bottom of the very last bag, the customs official found what he was searching for: a bottle of rare old French cognac.

"Nothing but clothes, you say?"

"That's what I said," replied the American.

"Well, what do you call this?" asked the official as he waved the bottle under the American's nose.

"That?" replied the American coldly. "Why, that's my nightcap."

BURLESQUE

A famous burlesque queen was robbed while staying in a hotel in Omaha. She was very unhappy about the loss of her favorite costume

—especially since it was such an important part of her act. Thinking to recover something for it, she cabled her insurance agent: "Gown lifted in Omaha hotel."

He wired back immediately: "Your policy doesn't cover that."

BUSINESS

A persistent salesman had been hounding the plant manager for nearly a week when he finally got him on the phone.

"I've been trying to see you all week," said the salesman.

"Make a date with my secretary," replied the busy manager.

"I did, and we had a wonderful time, but I still want to see *you*."

—●—

A woman who worked in the garment center wanted to buy a fur coat. A few blocks away from her office was a wholesale fur distributor, so she decided to go over and take a look around. She got to the place on her lunch hour, and finding it deserted, she wandered through the racks alone. Finally she came upon a rather harried-looking salesman who was loading big bales of fur pelts onto a cart.

"What do you want, lady?" he snapped impatiently.

"I'm looking for a Russian skunk," she replied.

"Stick around," he replied. "The boss will be back in a minute."

—●—

A harried young employee finally got up the courage to ask his boss for a raise.

"And just why should I give you a raise?" asked the boss.

"Because there are three companies after me," the employee replied.

"And who may they be?" inquired his employer.

"The gas company, the phone company, and the Acme Finance Company" was his weary reply.

—●—

Two "ladies of the evening" happened to meet one rainy night in a coffee shop near Times Square.

"Good grief, Belle," said her friend, "you look exhausted."

"I am," admitted the weary Belle. "If I'm not in bed by midnight, I'm going straight home!"

CABDRIVERS

A cabdriver slammed on his brakes and stopped dead in the middle of the street.

"What the hell do you think you're doing?" snarled one of the passengers as he picked himself up off the floor.

"I heard somebody yelling for me to stop," said the cabbie.

"Just keep driving," said the passenger. "She wasn't talking to you."

CALL GIRLS

A group of fraternity boys held a rather unique contest. Each boy contributed two dollars, the winner to take all the money for one night of passion in the arms of a famous New York City call girl. After the contest the winner, a rather inexperienced young man named Edgar, went to the call girl's apartment.

"That certainly is a lot of money," she said suspiciously as he handed her two hundred dollars. "Where did a kid like you get two hundred dollars?"

Edgar was embarrassed by the question and soon found himself blurting out the truth about the contest and how he had won the money, which could only be used to spend the night with her because she was so famous among the men of his fraternity.

"That is the most touching thing I've ever heard," she said sniffing. "To think that your fraternity brothers think so much of me. I'm going to do something I've never done before. I'm going to give you your money back."

And sure enough, she gave Edgar back his two dollars.

CAMPING

A city slicker went on his first camping trip in the wilds of Canada. He was extremely nervous and kept pestering his long-suffering guide with all sorts of foolish questions. He was particularly upset when the guide told him that much of the water in the area was not fit for drinking.

"But what should we do?" asked the city slicker.

"Just what we always do," replied his patient guide. "First we boil it, then we filter it, and then we add chlorine tablets to it."

"Then what?" asked the persistent city slicker.

"Then we go down to the lodge and drink beer."

CANNIBALS

A cannibal rushed into his village to spread the word that a hunting party had captured a politician.

"Good," said one of the cannibals enthusiastically, "I've always wanted to try a baloney sandwich."

"Does anyone here know what a cannibal is?" asked the teacher. No response. "John, you know what a cannibal is, don't you?"

"No, ma'am."

"Well," said the teacher, "if you were to eat your mother and your father, what would you be?"

"An orphan, ma'am" was John's irrefutable reply.

A cannibal chief was traveling to New York to speak on behalf of his tribe at the United Nations. He entered the dining room of the ocean liner and was seated by a steward who asked, "Would you like to see the menu?"

"No," said the chief, "just bring me the passenger list."

A little cannibal and his mother were standing in a clearing in the jungle when an airplane zoomed overhead.

"Mama," said the little cannibal, "is that airplane good to eat?"

"Well," replied his mother, "it's like a lobster. You only eat what's on the inside."

A group of cannibals attacked a mission but found that the missionaries had fled. The old chief was fascinated by a pile of magazines he found, especially one that had pictures of scantily clad women in the advertisements. Whenever he would come to a picture of a woman with very little on, he would tear out the page and eat it. Finally one of his sons noticed what he was doing and said, "Tell me, Dad, is that dehydrated stuff any good?"

CARNIVALS

"You know, George," said his wife as they strolled around the carnival, "I can't decide whether I should go to a palm-reader or a mind-reader."

"Well," said George, "I think you should go to the palm-reader."

"Why do you say that?"

"Because," replied George, "I'm *sure* you have a palm."

CATSKILLS

When asked what he thought of the newest resort hotel in the Catskills, Mr. Feinstein was overheard to say, "I never really saw too much of it. I went into the dining room my first day there and went snow-blind from the sour cream."

CHARITY

"Mommy," said little Johnny, "can I have a quarter for the man outside who is crying?"

"Certainly, dear," said his mother, "but what is he crying about?"

"Well," admitted Johnny, "he's crying, 'Ice cream, ice cream, twenty-five cents for ice cream.'"

—●—

A man was making his way home late one evening when another man moved out of the shadows and said, "Please, sir, won't you help a poor unfortunate fellow creature? I have no job, no home, no family." The first man was just about to brush past the fellow, but this next remark stopped him cold: "As a matter of fact, sir, all I have left in the whole world is this gun."

—●—

Old Mr. Patrick was visited by a representative of the Ladies' League who outlined the league's plans to open a free clinic for people too poor to afford medical treatment. Naturally, the league thought Mr. Patrick would want to contribute.

"Madam," said Mr. Patrick, "my sister has had a bad heart for years. My brother has been a cripple since he was fourteen years old. My wife is a semi-invalid, and my poor old mother has been in a nursing home for the last ten years. Now, really, madam, if I don't give a nickel to my own family, why should I give to strangers?"

—●—

An elegant society matron was stopped by a bum just as she was leaving one of the season's biggest charity balls.

"Lady," said the bum, "can you spare a poor man a dollar?"

"You must be out of your mind, you miserable ingrate," snapped the matron. "I spent two hundred fifty dollars for a ticket to the ball, one thousand five hundred dollars for my gown, and on top of that, I'm utterly exhausted from all that dancing. How dare you ask *me* for money when I did all *that* for you?"

CHEAPSKATES

Martha was complaining to her husband.

"Look at the old clothes I wear, you cheapskate. Why, if anyone came to visit us, they would think I was your cook."

"Not if they stayed for dinner" was her husband's terse reply.

—●—

"I'll say he's cheap! He's so cheap he would have asked for separate checks at the Last Supper."

—●—

Two bellhops were discussing the best tippers in the hotel.

"Watch out for that preacher's convention," cautioned the older bellhop.

"Are they cheap?" asked the younger man.

"Let me put it this way," answered the voice of experience. "Last year they showed up with the Ten Commandments in one hand and a ten-dollar bill in the other, and when they left, they hadn't broken either."

—●—

"You bum! You cheapskate!" shrieked Elsie to her spouse. "Look at the way I'm dressed. You never give me any money. You never let me buy any clothes. Just why won't you buy me a fur coat? You know I'm as cold as ice."

"That's why," replied her husband.

—●—

Angus was the most notorious miser in the neighborhood, but even the butcher was surprised when he came into the shop and asked for a quarter of a pound of steak.

"Angus," said the butcher, "you have eleven children. What on earth are you going to do with a quarter of a pound of steak?"

"Well," said Angus, "this steak isn't for eating. I just like to have the smell of steak cooking when we have company."

CIGARETTES

"May I have a cigarette?" said Joe.

"I thought you quit smoking," said his friend.

"Well, I'm in the process of quitting," admitted Joe. "Right now I'm in phase one."

"What's that?" inquired his friend.

"I've quit buying."

—●—

Two friends were talking about their old pal Fred. "You know," said one, "Fred was worried about his health. He even quit smoking."

"Didn't you hear?" asked the other. "Fred died a week ago."

"No!" came the shocked reply. "Was it cigarettes?"

"In a way," admitted his friend. "He was run over by a tobacco truck."

CLOTHES

I went out to dinner last night with a girl whose dress was cut so low that I had to look under the table to see what she was wearing.

—●—

Lola was showing off her new mink coat to the rest of the girls in the chorus. "Gee, that's some coat," said her friend Maxine. "Is it really yours?"

"It sure is, honey," replied Lola with a smile. "Of course, I'm still making nightly payments on it."

—●—

"Darling," cooed the wife. "Just wait until you see the beautiful surprise I bought for your birthday."
"I can hardly wait, dear."
"Good," she replied. "Just give me a second, and I'll go and put it on."

—●—

Always remember, "If at first you don't succeed, try, try again." Then if you still aren't getting anywhere, try offering her a mink coat.

—●—

Teen-age boy on phone to girl friend: "Gee, Cindy, I'd love to take you to the dance next Friday. Is it formal, or can I wear my own clothes?"

—●—

"Charles," demanded his wife, "do you think I am going to wear this old muskrat coat all my life?"
"Why not, dear?" he replied. "The muskrats do."

—●—

"Do you mind if I try that dress on in the window?" asked the customer.
"Not at all, madam," replied the clerk, "but wouldn't you rather use the dressing room?"

COLLEGE

Mr. Thomas was winding up a business trip in a town that was just twenty miles from his eldest son's college. Thinking to surprise him, Mr. Thomas rented a car and drove off in the general direction of the college. However, due to his unfamiliarity with the area and some bad directions from the local gas-station attendant, Mr. Thomas got lost, and it wasn't until the wee hours of the morning that he pulled up in front of his son's fraternity house. Utterly exhausted, Mr. Thomas hoped his son might be able to put him up for what remained of the night. He parked his car and walked up to the fraternity-house door.

He rang the bell several times before someone opened a second-story window and a sleepy voice called down, "What do you want?"

"Does Henry Thomas live here?" inquired the weary parent.

"Yeah, he lives here" came the terse reply. "Just dump him on the porch."

—●—

Two friends were comparing letters from their kids in college.

"When my son writes to me, his letters send me to the dictionary," admitted one parent.

"You're lucky," said the other. "When my daughter writes to me, her letters send me to the bank."

—●—

A college student decided that he wanted to get married, but unfortunately he had no money and no job, so he decided to have a talk with his father.

"Dad," he said, "do you believe that two can live as cheaply as one?"

"I certainly do, my boy. As a matter of fact I know they can. Right now your mother and I live as cheaply as you do."

—●—

An out-of-towner mistook the local mental hospital for the local college. The guard set him straight and gave him directions.

As he got back into his car, the stranger said, "Come to think of it, there isn't much difference between a college and a mental hospital these days."

"Well," replied the guard, "I can think of one difference. You've got to show *improvement* to get out of *this* place."

—●—

A very staid Boston law firm decided to get some young blood into the firm, so they advertised for a lawyer who was either "a Harvard graduate or the equivalent."

A few days later they received a letter from a Yale graduate who inquired, "When you say 'equivalent' do you want two Princeton men, or would a Yale graduate working half-time do?"

—●—

Two fraternity brothers were talking.

"I really love Mary Lou," said the first. "She's the kind of girl I'd like to take home to Mother."

"Well, why don't you?" asked his buddy.

"Because I can't trust my father" came the honest reply.

COMEDIANS

You know, every time I get up before an audience to tell a few jokes I am reminded of that old line, "Something old, something new, something borrowed, something blue." I can't think of a better way to describe my act.

COMPETITION

A rooster wandered out of his own barnyard and over onto the next farm, where he came upon an ostrich egg. Amazed by the size of the egg, he waited until dark and then spent the whole night carefully pushing and pulling the egg over into his own domain. The next morning he let out a crow to wake up the hens, and when they came out into the barnyard, they found the rooster leaning nonchalantly on the ostrich egg. The hens gathered around in amazement, and the rooster was heard to say, "Up until now, girls, I haven't wanted to complain. But I thought it was about time you got a look at our competitor's model."

CONCEIT

You know, my brother-in-law is so conceited that on his last birthday he sent a letter of congratulations to his mother.

CONVENTIONS

The members of the lodge were trying to decide whether or not they should take their wives with them to their annual convention. The arguments from the floor raged on until one member sort of summed it up for the con side.

"Look," he said, "taking your wife to a convention like this is like going hunting with the game warden."

COOKING

A new bride placed a casserole dish in front of her husband and said, "My mother taught me to cook only two dishes—chili con carne and lemon pie. I hope you like it."

"It's fine, dear," said her loving husband as he tasted the concoction. "But which is it?"

Husband to wife while sampling her "homemade" soup: "Am I supposed to eat it or dip arrows in it?"

"Darling," said the tactful new husband, "this meat loaf certainly tastes *different*."

"Oh," replied his bride, "I thought I might have ruined it. It got a little burned, but I fixed it."

"What did you do?" asked her husband.

"I just added a little sunburn cream."

COST OF LIVING

It is still true that two can live as cheaply as one. But nowadays they both have to work to earn enough money to do it.

Mr. Bernbaum wanted to do a little remodeling, so he called in a housepainter and asked for an estimate. The painter looked the house over and said he'd take the job for seven hundred dollars.

"Seven hundred dollars!" cried the outraged homeowner. "Why, I wouldn't pay Van Gogh that much."

"Oh, yeah?" replied the painter. "If he does the job for any less, he'll have to cross a picket line first."

COUNTRY FOLKS

"Tell me, Jasper," asked one of the old farmers in the country store, "why do you treat that fellow with such respect?"

"Well, Zeb," replied the owner, "it's because he's one of our early settlers."

"Can't be, Jasper. That young fellow isn't more than twenty-five years old."

"Not that kind of settler, Zeb. I mean he pays his bills on the first of every month."

—•—

Two old farmers were talking.

"How's your son Abner?" asked the first.

"Just fine," replied Abner's father. "He's a real hard worker, that boy."

"Yes," agreed the first farmer, "he certainly seems ambitious."

"Ambitious!" replied Abner's father. "Why, that boy is planning on being so rich that he already treats me like some kind of poor relation."

—•—

A clever thief devoted himself to robbing the houses of religious people because he felt that they would not be moved to violence over the loss of worldly goods. One night, however, he met his match. The sounds of his ransacking the living room aroused the old Quaker whose house it was. The old man got out of bed, picked up his hunting rifle, and made his way downstairs, where he confronted the thief.

"My friend," he said, "not for anything would I do thee harm, but thee are standing where I am about to shoot."

The thief has not been seen in those parts since.

—•—

"What's wrong, Effie?" asked her maw. "Aren't you and Luke getting along?"

"It ain't exactly that, Maw," she replied. "It's just that sometimes I don't think Luke loves me anymore."

"What makes you think that, child?" asked her maw.

"Well, the other night Luke came home and said he had bought some things for the person he loved best in all the world."

"What did he buy?" asked her maw.

"A plug of chewing tobacco and a jug of moonshine" was the sad reply.

—•—

"How's the wife?" inquired the old mountaineer of his harried friend.

"Not too good," he replied sadly. "The doctor says the only thing that will do her any good is a long rest where she can get the sea breezes."

"Why don't you take her down to the Gulf?" asked the old-timer.

"Can't afford it," admitted his friend. "But every night I've been fanning her with a dead fish."

— ● —

A smart-aleck tourist engaged an old Vermont farmer in conversation. "Tell me, old-timer, where did all these rocks come from?"

"Well, son, I figure a glacier brought them."

"Oh," replied the tourist, "where's that glacier now?"

"Went back for more rocks, I reckon."

— ● —

The judge was having trouble getting an account of just what had caused the free-for-all at the barn dance. He finally called old Abner to the stand.

"Now, Abner," said the judge, "I want you to tell the court in your own words just what started this fight."

"Well, Judge, it was like this. Bill McCoy asked Zeke Hawkins's wife for a dance. Old Zeke didn't take kindly to the way they was a'lookin' at each other, so he called Bill a mangy, no-account woman-stealing so and so. That kinda made Bill mad, so he whacks old Zeke across the face with an ax handle. Zeke fell right into Mrs. Jethro's lap, and this made Mr. Jethro mad. So he ups and hits old Bill with a saddle, which was just lying there on the ground. That made Ben Taylor mad, on account of it was his saddle, and he took a swing at Mr. Jethro. In the meantime Zeke and Bill were wrasslin' around, and pretty soon it seemed like a lot of folks were getting kind of mad. Old Jed Stevens tried to stop it by firing a couple of shots, but one of his bullets hit Ma Banes, and that caused some excitement, and folks just naturally commenced to fight."

"I see," said the judge. "Case dismissed."

— ● —

"My wooden leg sure gave me a lot of pain last night," complained old Clay Taylor as he limped around the general store.

"That's too bad. What seems to be wrong with it?" inquired a sympathetic customer.

"Oh, nothing's wrong with the leg. It's just that last night my wife hit me over the head with it."

—●—

"Doc, I want you to treat a bullet wound in my son-in-law's leg."

"Certainly, Jed, but you'll have to tell me how it happened so I can report it."

"Well, Doc, I shot him."

"Now, why did you shoot your son-in-law, Jed?"

"To make sure he'd be my son-in-law."

—●—

Two women were discussing the problem of getting their husbands up in the morning.

"How do you get Zeke out of bed in the morning?"

"Oh, he ain't no trouble at all. I just open the bedroom door and let the cat in."

"Does that get him up?"

"Sure does," she replied. "He sleeps with the dog."

—●—

A particular backwoods community was notorious for the way it ran its preachers out of town. Not one clergyman had ever lasted more than a month. Finally a young minister, fresh out of school, was sent to the town, and strangely enough, he was still there six months later. His superiors began to feel guilty, so they sent one of their number out to see how he was doing. The young minister, it seemed, was doing just fine—at least according to the local mayor.

"Folks out here don't really want any preacher at all, and he's about as close as we're likely to get," he explained.

—●—

Lucy and her grandma went to church every Sunday. The old lady was very religious and boasted that she hadn't missed a Sunday in forty years. You can imagine Lucy's surprise when the old girl got up and walked out in the middle of the new preacher's sermon. Lucy took off after the old lady and caught up with her about two miles up the road.

"Gran, what on earth made you do such a thing?" demanded Lucy.

"That sermon of his was over!" snapped Granny.

"Why, he was only half through. He done preached against gamblin', and he done preached against gossipin', and he was just startin' on drinkin' when you got up and left."

"That's what I mean," said the old lady. "He was done preachin'. He was just startin' in on meddlin'.''

The preacher stopped to visit Ephraim on his ninety-eighth birthday. The old man was sitting on the front porch rocking away and looking pretty happy for a man of his age.

"You look mighty pleased with yourself, Ephraim," said the preacher.

"Sure am, preacher. I'm ninety-eight today, and I don't have an enemy in this world."

"That's wonderful, Ephraim. How do you figure you managed it?" asked the preacher, thinking he might get an inspirational thought for Sunday's sermon.

"Outlived every damn one of them" came the smug reply.

An old farmer had three daughters. When the oldest girl married, she moved to Twin Cities, Minnesota, and soon gave birth to a beautiful set of twin boys. Her sister married shortly thereafter, and she and her husband took up residence in Three Rivers, Ontario. Pretty soon she gave birth to triplets. The youngest sister got herself engaged, but after almost a year she still refused to set the date for the wedding. Her father grew concerned and finally demanded that she stop procrastinating and set the date.

"If you love that boy, you'll marry him this spring, or you won't marry him at all!"

"But, Pa," she wailed, "I really do love Fred, but he keeps talking about moving to the Thousand Islands."

An old banker was telling his grandson how he got his start by opening a bank in the hills of Tennessee.

"T'weren't hard, boy. One day I hung up a sign that said 'Bank.' A fella came along and gave me fifty dollars. Next thing I knew another fella gave me two hundred dollars. By the end of the first week I had so much confidence I even put in twenty dollars of my own money."

—●—

An old mountain man spent most of his day just sitting on the front porch, whittling and rocking and taking an occasional nip from his jug. One afternoon his neighbor came to visit, and the two of them spent the afternoon peacefully. Late in the afternoon the old mountaineer informed his visitor that he'd best be on his way, since the hour was growing late.

"How can you tell what time it is, Jake? You don't even own a watch."

"True enough," replied Jake. "But I can see that it's time for you to be getting on home by the shadow on the floor."

"Is that so? Well, what time is it?"

"It's about three planks 'til suppertime."

—●—

A mountain man and his dog were walking through the fields one day when they happened to meet the new schoolmaster. While they were talking, the old dog pointed three times to different spots, and each time old Matthew fired his gun where the dog had pointed. But not once was there any indication that there was a bird where the dog had pointed. After the fourth shot the schoolmaster couldn't contain himself any longer.

"Matt," he asked, "why do you shoot if you know there aren't any birds?"

"Well, son, it's like this. This old dog and me, we've had some mighty good times together. Now, his nose ain't what it used to be, but his spirit is just as strong as ever. I couldn't hardly live with myself if I was to go and call him a liar after all these years."

—●—

Zeke brought his family to town one Sunday just to see the sights. His two sons were so busy gaping at the sights that they forgot to look where they were going and ran headlong into a priest, who was wearing a cast on his foot. Zeke rushed over to apologize for his clumsy offspring, and he and the priest fell into conversation.

"What did you do to your foot, Father?"

"I slipped and broke it in the bathtub," replied the priest.

Later, on their way home, one of Zeke's sons asked, "Pa, what's a bathtub?"

"I couldn't say, son," replied his father. "I ain't Catholic."

—•—

"You sure are a pretty gal, Peggy Sue," sighed young Jethro. "And you sing real good. I bet you sing good enough to go on the stage."

"Why, Jethro, you know Pa would never stand for such a thing," she replied. "He don't hold with going to visit the city, much less letting me go to work there."

"Why, don't he trust you?"

"Well, it ain't that exactly," admitted Peggy Sue. "He trusts me, all right. He just don't trust nobody else."

—•—

Zeb and his wife, Addie, had had a reputation for being the stingiest couple in the hills. Zeb died a few years back, and his kin was downright embarrassed about the way Addie took on about the cost of the funeral. She even insisted on having the coffin closed so she wouldn't have to pay the undertaker for a room to hold the viewing.

A few years later Addie got sick, and it looked like she was going to meet Zeb in the hereafter. Addie called her only friend to her side and made her promise to see to the funeral.

"Promise you'll bury me in my black silk dress," she said weakly. "But you may as well cut the material out of the back of the skirt. It's good material, and it surely is a sin to waste it."

"Now, Addie," replied her friend, "I just couldn't. When you and Zeb walk through those pearly gates, you surely don't want to go with no back to your dress."

"Don't give it another thought," replied Addie. "They'll all be looking at Zeb anyhow."

"Why do you say that?"

"Because I buried him without his pants."

—•—

"I sure am sorry to hear about your daughter," said the preacher sympathetically.

"It never would have happened if we hadn't taken her to the county fair," her mother said, sniffing. "We warned her against the sins of gambling."

"Perhaps I am a little confused," said the minister. "I thought Betty Jo was about to become an unwed mother."

"You ain't confused," admitted her ma.

"But what's that got to do with gambling?" inquired the minister.

"It never would have happened if she hadn't taken a chance on that rug."

—●—

Ma Benson stopped into the general store for some hairpins.

"I want invisible hairpins," she insisted to the storekeeper.

When he brought her hairpins, she was not convinced.

"Are you sure these hairpins are invisible?" she demanded.

"Ma," said the storekeeper, "I'll tell you how invisible these hairpins are. We ran out of them last Friday, and so far this week I've sold three dollars' worth."

—●—

Up in the hills of Tennessee a group of doctors opened a free clinic. One local woman took full advantage of the clinic's maternity ward. She had six kids before the clinic opened, and she appeared once a year in the spring to give birth to another.

As she was leaving the clinic with her eleventh child, her doctor remarked good-naturedly, "I suppose I'll be seeing you again next year around this time."

"Oh, no!" replied the woman firmly. "While I was here this time, I was talkin' to that new nurse of yours. Now I know what's causin' em."

—●—

A couple of hillbillies appeared in the bridal department of a fashionable department store in New Orleans. The manager took them in hand, but when she heard what they wanted to buy, she assured them that her store did not stock "maternity wedding gowns."

"As a matter of fact," she said definitely, "I would be willing to bet that there isn't a store in the entire state of Louisiana that carries such an item."

"That so?" mused one of the would-be customers. " 'Bout time you folks caught up. We got 'em back home in Tennessee."

—●—

The old mountain man was watching the storekeeper unwrap a shipment of brightly colored men's pajamas.

"What's that?" he asked.

"Pajamas," replied the storekeeper.

"What are they for?"

"You wear them at night," the storekeeper explained. "Would you like to buy a pair?"

"Nope," said the mountain man. "Don't go no place at night except to bed."

—●—

Old Eb was the biggest skinflint in the county. So when his son started courting Ellie May, he was naturally concerned about the cost. One night his son came home to find Eb waiting up for him.

"Can't you sleep, Pa?"

"No, boy, I can't. I keep thinking about how you're out spending money on such foolishness."

"Why, Pa, you shouldn't worry. We spent only a dollar tonight."

Even Eb had to admit that that wasn't so bad.

"It was all she had," said his son.

—●—

Miss Thelma Perkins and her sister Alma were the only two women for three hundred miles up in the mountains of Carolina. And it was a lonely life. They had each other to talk to, but they never did have another woman to talk about.

—●—

"My pa is the best shot in the county," said Minnie Pearl to the young man lying at her side.

"Well, what does that make me?" he inquired.

"My fiancé" was her decisive reply.

—●—

Old Zeb was complaining about a freeloading cousin of his who came for a visit and was still with him six months later.

"You know," said Zeb to his sympathetic listeners, "I didn't mind when he moved in to the best bedroom. It didn't bother me too much when he started wearing my clothes. I didn't even get mad when he started courtin' my gal. But this morning when I asked him if it wasn't about time for him to be gettin' on home and he laughed at me with my own teeth, that was the last straw."

—•—

Two men from the Ozarks came to the big city and decided to visit a museum. They made their way into the Egyptian wing and stood staring at a mummy case bearing the inscription 1256 B.C.

"What do you make of them numbers, Zeke?"

"Well," replied the mountaineer, "cain't rightly say 'lessen it's the license number of the car that killed him."

COURTESY

A very sexy woman boarded a crowded bus and finding no empty seats, asked a well-dressed gentleman to give her his seat.

"Ordinarily I would never ask," she said, "but you see, I'm pregnant."

Looking over her superb figure, the gentleman was moved to comment, "You're welcome to the seat, but you certainly don't look pregnant."

"Well," she replied with a smile, "it's only been about fifteen minutes."

COWBOYS

Why did the cowboy put a saddle on the porcupine?
Because he didn't want to ride him bareback.

CREDIT

A man who was applying for a loan was asked, "Do you usually live within your income?"

"Good Lord, no," he replied. "It's all I can do to live within my credit."

—•—

A bill collector spent weeks trying to track down a woman who had bought a couch on time and had not made the required payments. He finally found her at home one afternoon and after getting into her apartment demanded, "Okay, lady, what about the next installment on that couch?"

She thought about it for a minute and replied, "All right. I guess that's better than giving you money for it."

CRIME

The mayor has just *got* to do something about the crime rate in this city. It's gotten so bad that after dark even the *muggers* travel in pairs.

—●—

Two men held up a bank. They cleaned out the cash drawers and then herded the tellers and clerks into the vault. They were getting ready to make their getaway when one of the tellers whispered, "Hey, buddy, would you do me a favor?"
One of the robbers said, "What's on your mind, pal?"
"Would you mind taking the books, too? I'm five thousand short."

—●—

A man whose store had been robbed the night before was having coffee with a detective who had been assigned to the case. "I'm sorry to hear about this," said the detective sympathetically. "Did you lose a great deal?"
The storekeeper shrugged and said, "Quite a bit, but it could have been a lot worse. It was lucky the robber didn't break in the night before last."
"Why's that?" asked the detective.
"Well," replied the storekeeper logically, "yesterday morning I marked everything down forty percent."

DEBTS

Mr. Levy, a very fine kosher butcher, passed away. On the evening of the day he died he appeared at the gates of hell, demanding to see the landlord.
Lucifer himself opened the gates and said, "Levy, what are you doing here? You're supposed to be in heaven. You trying to give my place a good name?"
"No," replied Levy, "I know I should be in heaven. But before I go I wanted to collect a few old debts."
"I see," said the devil. "But you're dead. What are you doing here?"

"Well, I'll tell you," said the butcher. "Every time I tried to collect these debts while I was alive those people always told me that *this* is where I should go."

—•—

Mr. Harvey and his brother-in-law were having lunch together. "You know," said Mr. Harvey, "every time I see you I can't get over how much you remind me of George Kirby."

"But that's ridiculous," exclaimed his brother-in-law. "George Kirby and I have nothing in common."

"On the contrary," replied Mr. Harvey. "For one thing, you *both* owe me money."

DECISIONS

"I demand an explanation, and I want the truth!" shouted the irate husband upon discovering his wife in bed with his best friend.

"Make up your mind, George," she calmly replied. "You can't have both."

DEMOCRACY

In a democracy every man is free to choose his own form of government—blonde, brunette, or redhead.

DEPARTMENT STORES

A little old lady came through the revolving doors into one of New York's biggest department stores and was shocked when a brass band started playing. She was even more startled when the store manager rushed up, pinned an orchid on her lapel, and started pumping her hand up and down while photographers snapped pictures of the whole thing.

"Congratulations, ma'am," he shouted over the din. "You are this store's millionth customer." TV cameras zoomed in for a close-up, and someone stuck a microphone in her hand. "Tell me," continued the manager, "just why did you come to our store this afternoon?"

"Well, to tell you the truth," said the lady with a shy smile, "I'm just on my way to the ladies' room."

DIETS

"Hey, Harry, how's your wife getting along on her diet?" asked one of the boys at the bar.

"Terrific," admitted Harry. "Last night she disappeared completely."

—●—

Sam bumped into his old friend Joe on a busy street and very nearly passed him by without even recognizing him. Joe looked awful. His face was thin and drawn, he had bags under his eyes, and his clothes just hung on him.

"My God, Joe, what happened? Have you been sick?"

"No" came the weary reply. "My wife is on a diet."

DIPLOMACY

I know a man who couldn't care less about the war between the Arabs and the Jews. He's an old farmer who lives right on the Israeli-Arab border. But, then, why should he worry? His name is Aga Cohen.

—●—

"What advice would you give to a young man entering diplomatic service?" the reporter asked the retiring diplomat.

"I would advise him to remain in top physical condition," replied the weary peacemaker.

"Why do you feel that this is valuable for a diplomat?" queried the newsman.

"Because, my boy, we diplomats are usually either straddling an issue or dodging one."

—●—

With both parents convinced that each was a great violinist there were bound to be a few tense moments. One evening a tactless visitor asked little Ralph who *he* thought was the best violinist in the whole world. Without a moment's hesitation the child replied, "Heifetz."

—●—

"Daddy, what's diplomacy?" asked little Bill, just home from school.

"Well, son, it's like this," replied his dad. "If I were to say to your mother, 'Your face would stop a clock,' that would be stupidity. But if I were to say, 'When I look at you, time stands still,' *that* is diplomacy!"

—•—

Mr. Garfield, an extremely successful if somewhat pompous businessman, found himself seated next to an Oriental gentleman one evening at a charity banquet.

When the consommé was served, Mr. Garfield inquired solicitously, "Likee soupee?"

The Oriental nodded his assent.

After dinner the master of ceremonies announced the guest speaker. The Oriental rose, walked to the podium, and delivered a very informative speech on Communist China's place in the world market. His knowledge of the subject was enhanced by his impeccable, clearly enunciated Oxford English.

When he was finished, he returned to the table, smiled broadly, and inquired of the stunned Mr. Garfield, "Likee speechee?"

DISCRETION

"Daddy, my teacher says I shouldn't fight so much. She says I should use my discretion. Only I don't know if I've got any, 'cause I don't know what it is."

"Well, son," replied his dad, gazing at his son's latest black eye, "in your case I guess discretion is knowing when to close your eyes to an insult before somebody closes them for you."

DIVORCE

"I can't stand him for one more minute! If I don't do something soon, I will go insane. He gets drunk, spends all our money on horses and other women, and if he comes home at all, it's just to change his clothes."

"Well, madam," admitted the lawyer, "it certainly looks as though you have grounds for divorce."

"Divorce! I should say not! I've lived with that bum for thirty years, and *now* I should make him happy?"

—•—

Overheard on a plane landing in Nevada:
"Just what are the grounds for divorce in this state?"

"Are you married?"

"Yes."

"Then you've got grounds for divorce."

—●—

"My dear," gushed Mrs. Wyatt, "how simply awful. I just heard about your poor husband going bankrupt. I feel so sorry for him."

"So do I," sighed Mrs. Maitland. "He's going to miss me so."

—●—

"Isn't it amazing!" gushed the bride to her favorite uncle as they danced at the wedding reception. "They just murmur a few words over you, and you're married."

"Yes," agreed her thrice-married uncle. "And a few words murmured in your sleep, and you're divorced!"

—●—

"Not only am I going to grant your wife a divorce," snapped the judge, "I am going to give her one hundred dollars a week in alimony."

"That's mighty nice of you, Judge. I'll try to slip her a few bucks myself from time to time."

—●—

The judge brought the court to order and inquired as to the nature of the case before the bench. The shapely defendant wanted a divorce.

"On what grounds?" asked the judge.

"Infidelity," she replied.

"Infidelity!" replied the disbelieving judge as he gazed appreciatively at the lovely young woman before him. "What makes you think your husband was unfaithful?"

"Well, your honor, for one thing, I'm sure he isn't the father of our child."

—●—

A man went to see his lawyer about getting a divorce.

"How much do you charge for handling a case like mine?" he asked.

"I really don't like to handle divorce cases," replied his attorney. "Why do you want to get a divorce?"

"Because I want to marry my wife's sister."

"Now, a case like that could get pretty messy. It might cost you as much as a thousand dollars. Why don't you go home and think it over."

So the man went home, and the next day he called his lawyer.

"I've talked the whole thing over with my best friend," he said. "I've decided not to get a divorce after all."

"That's just fine," said his lawyer. "Tell me, what did your friend say that made you change your mind?"

"Well, he tells me he's been out with my wife and her sister, too, and there ain't a nickel's worth of difference between them."

DOCTORS

Max went to the doctor for his yearly checkup and was greatly relieved when the doctor gave him a clean bill of health.

"Just remember one thing, Max. Your body is your home. So keep it clean and neat."

"I got ya, Doc. I'll call in a woman twice a week."

—•—

A man went to see his doctor and during the examination confessed that his one goal in life was to live to be a hundred. The doctor told him that he would have to quit smoking and drinking and give up women, too.

The man seemed interested and said, "If I do all that, will I really live to be a hundred?"

"I can't guarantee that you'll live to *be* a hundred," admitted the doctor, "but it will sure *seem* that way."

—•—

A man who had just undergone a very complicated operation kept complaining about a bump on his head and a terrible headache. Since his operation had been an intestinal one, there was no earthly reason why he should be complaining of a headache. Finally his nurse, fearing that the man might be suffering from some postoperative shock, spoke to the doctor about it.

"Don't worry about a thing, nurse," the doctor assured her. "He really does have a bump on his head. About halfway through the operation we ran out of anesthetic."

A man went to see his doctor because he was suffering from a miserable cold. His doctor prescribed some pills, but they didn't help. On his next visit the doctor gave him a shot, but that didn't do any good. On his third visit the doctor told the man to go home and take a hot bath. As soon as he was finished bathing he was to throw open all the windows and stand in the draft.

"But, Doc," protested the patient, "if I do that, I'll get pneumonia."

"I know," said his physician. "I can cure pneumonia."

A busy executive pushed himself too hard, and his health began to suffer. Finally he went to see his doctor for a complete physical. A few days later he went back for the results of his test.

"Tell me the truth," he said to the doctor. "Was it bad? What did my electrocardiogram show?"

"Well, let me put it this way," said his diplomatic physician. "If I were to put your chart on a player piano, I'm afraid the tune would be 'Nearer, My God, to Thee.'"

A man went to see the doctor because of a pain in his back.

The doctor examined him and asked, "Didn't you have a pain like this before?"

"I sure did, Doc. Have you figured out what it is yet?"

"No, but I'm sure of one thing," replied the doctor.

"What's that, Doc?"

"You've got it again."

A doctor was awakened at four in the morning by a caller who demanded to know how much he charged for a house call.

"Twenty-five dollars," muttered the sleepy physician.

"How much is an office visit?" demanded the caller.

"Fifteen dollars."

"Okay, Doc," said the caller. "I'll meet you in your office in fifteen minutes."

—•—

A beautiful young WAC went to the base doctor and said, "Doctor, you must help me. I think I need an operation."

"Major?" asked the doctor with concern.

"No," she said with a sigh, "Lieutenant."

—•—

A doctor and his wife were having dinner out one evening when a stunning redhead who was being seated at a nearby table recognized the doctor and waved at him.

Noticing the look his wife was giving him, he said in a soothing tone, "Now, dear, I met her professionally."

"Really," she snapped. "Yours or hers?"

—•—

An old country doctor found his work load too heavy and managed to persuade a young doctor to share his practice.

"Just remember, son," cautioned the older man, "these are simple country folk. They don't have much of a way with words, and sometimes they won't be able to describe their symptoms accurately. But you just keep your eyes open, and you'll be able to diagnose their ailments with no trouble at all."

That very evening the two doctors were called to the aid of a beautiful young girl who lay in a stupor. The older doctor took her pulse while the younger man tried to take her temperature. His efforts only seemed to upset her, and her violent tossing and turning caused him to drop the thermometer. He bent over and picked it up and put it back in his bag. He waved the older doctor aside and whispered a few words into the young woman's ear. Whatever he said seemed to soothe her, and the two men went on their way. When they got into the car, the old doctor demanded to know what the young man had said to the patient.

"I simply told her that she would have to cut down on her political activity."

"Now, that is ridiculous!" exclaimed the old practitioner. "She was practically in a coma, and you thought it was politics? You are a fool."

"No, sir, I just did what you told me to do. I just kept my eyes open."

"Now, what is that supposed to mean?" demanded the irate physician.

"Well, when I bent over to pick up the thermometer, I saw the mayor under the bed."

—●—

Dr. Martin called his answering service and was told that a man named Fred had called his number and left word that he couldn't live without him. The operator was very upset because Fred had hung up before she could get his last name or his address or even give him the hospital's emergency number.

"Don't worry about it, operator," said the doctor calmly. "It isn't me Fred can't live without—it's my daughter."

—●—

Two old men were arguing the merits of their doctors.

The first one said, "I don't trust your fancy doctor. He treated old Jake Waxman for a kidney ailment for nearly a year, and then Jake died of a liver ailment."

"So what makes you think your doctor is any better?" asked his friend.

"Because when my doctor treats you for a kidney ailment, you can be sure you'll *die* of a kidney ailment."

—●—

Overheard at the doctor's office:

"Miss LaRue, you have acute appendicitis!"

"Doctor, really, I appreciate the compliment, but I came for an examination."

—●—

"Doctor, you've got to help me," said the patient.

"What seems to be the trouble?"

"I have a couple of nickels caught in my ear and——"

"Good Lord, man. How long have you had them there?"

"About a year."

"Why didn't you come and see me sooner?" asked the doctor.

"To tell you the truth, Doc, up until now I didn't need the money."

—•—

"You've just got to slow down, Harry," said the doctor. "You'll be dead in a year if you don't give up your wild ways."

"But, Doctor," said Harry. "I'm a man of regular habits."

"Is that so?" said the doctor. "Then how come I saw you out at four this morning with a girl who looked young enough to be your daughter?"

"Like I said, Doc, that's one of my regular habits."

—•—

A group of medical students were listening to a lecture. The lecturer decided to prove his point by dropping a couple of worms into a jar of alcohol. The worms were dead within seconds.

"Now, as you can see, gentlemen, this is the effect of alcohol on the lesser organisms. Now, what do you suppose this proves in the case of man?"

One of the students thought for a moment and then concluded, "Any man who drinks won't get worms."

—•—

A woman called her doctor frantically.

"Doctor," she gasped, "my husband fell asleep with his mouth open, and a mouse ran into his mouth."

"Be calm," said the doctor. "Try waving a piece of cheese in front of his mouth. Perhaps the mouse will come out."

"All right," said the woman, "but I'll try it with a piece of mackerel."

"Don't be ridiculous," said the doctor. "A mouse won't come out for a piece of mackerel."

"True," replied the concerned wife, "but the mouse won't come out at all if we don't get the cat out of there first."

—•—

A woman rushed into her doctor's office.

"Doctor," she exclaimed, "you must help me. My husband swallowed an alarm clock."

"Well, bring him in," said the doctor.

"He's home asleep," she replied.

"Well, for heaven's sake, why are you here?"

"Because he bit me when I tried to wind it."

—•—

Doctors can work miracles these days. Why, my doctor can even foretell the future. About eight months ago I broke my ankle. My doctor rushed right over, taped up my ankle, drove me to the hospital himself, supervised my X rays, put a cast on my foot himself, and then told me I'd be walking in no time.

He was absolutely right. I was walking by the end of the month. After his bill came in, I had to sell my car to pay him.

—•—

Sally, a beautiful but dumb blonde, went to visit her doctor.

"Okay, Sally, I'll examine you now," said the doctor. "You can get undressed now."

"Okay, Doc," said Sally with a blush. "But you first."

—•—

A man went to the doctor and complained that he wasn't feeling well.

"Strip to the waist," said the doctor, "and when I hit you on the back, I want you to cough."

This process went on for nearly half an hour. Finally the doctor told him to get dressed and said, "Just one question. How long have you had this cough?"

—•—

A woman asked her doctor what her husband should take when he was run-down.

"The license number" was the physician's instant reply.

—•—

"I'm not sure I can diagnose your case," said the doctor. "I'm afraid, Mr. Beamish, that it's drink."

"That's okay, Doc. I'll come back when you're sober."

—•—

"Doctor," gushed the young woman as she entered his office, "I can't begin to tell you what you've done for me!"

"Why, thank you, madam," said the doctor, "but I must confess I cannot remember what it was I treated you for."

"Oh, no, Doctor, not me. My husband was your patient, and I was his sole heir."

—●—

A woman went to her doctor and complained of a severe earache. He examined her ear and found a piece of string dangling from it. The doctor began pulling the string. He pulled and pulled until he had a ball of string of an alarming size. Finally to his utter amazement a big bouquet of flowers fell out of her ear.

"Good Lord!" exclaimed the doctor, "where did this come from?"

"How should I know," replied his patient. "Why don't you read the card?"

—●—

After completing his annual physical checkup, Mr. Harris was informed that he was going to need a very expensive operation and then at least a year to recuperate. Mr. Harris was desperate.

"I just can't afford an operation like that. Especially if it means that I will be out of work for a year. Isn't there something else you can do for me?"

"Well," said the doctor, "I could always have your X rays retouched."

—●—

"I am going to operate on Mrs. Blackstone," said the doctor.

"What is your fee?" asked her next of kin.

"One thousand dollars," replied the doctor.

"What does she have?"

"One thousand dollars."

—●—

"Isn't it amazing how much those two beautiful girls resemble each other?" said the handsome gentleman to his dinner partner.

"Not at all" was her catty reply. "They both went to the same plastic surgeon."

—●—

Modern medical techniques are wonderful. I went to a doctor who told me he wanted to take out my appendix. I was a little concerned, but he told me not to worry. He said that with today's methods I would be sitting up three hours after the operation, and if everything went as planned, I'd be on my feet the next day and out of the hospital the day after. I'm all for being efficient, but this guy was in such a hurry that when they brought me into the operating room, he didn't even want me to lie down.

DOGS

Two skiers found themselves stranded halfway down the slope by a blinding snowstorm. However, they were rescued by a huge Saint Bernard who came bounding toward them with a keg of brandy strapped to his collar.

"Thank God," cried the first skier as he spotted the dog. "It's man's best friend."

"It sure is," agreed his companion. "And look at the size of the dog who's carrying it."

—●—

An overbearing but extremely rich matron wanted to buy a dog. She searched through the most fashionable pet shops but never found anything to suit her. One day she was driving through the country when she happened to see a sign nailed to a barn which said, PUPPIES FOR SALE. She had her driver turn into the driveway, and it was there she confronted the farmer. She carefully inspected the dogs and was quite taken with the litter, even though they were plain, ordinary mutts. However, she wasn't quite satisfied.

"I really do like this little dog," she admitted to the farmer, "but his legs are too short." The farmer took the dog and set him down.

"I don't know what makes you say that, ma'am," he drawled. "All four of 'em touch the ground."

DRINKING

"Poor Max," said his sister. "Marriage hasn't helped him a bit. He still drinks too much."

"Yes," agreed her husband, "but for different reasons. He used to drink *for* pleasure. Now he drinks *from* pain."

—●—

A teetotaler and a drinking man were debating the relative merits of alcohol.

"For one thing," said the drinker, "I'll wager that plain, ordinary water has killed more people than liquor ever has."

"How do you figure that?" asked the teetotaler.

"Well, first look at all the folks who died in the Flood."

A drunk decided to give an old college buddy he hadn't seen in years a call. He got the operator to put the call through, and it was only as he was listening to the ring that he realized that it was four o'clock in the morning.

"Gee, buddy," he said to his sleepy friend, "I hope I didn't disturb you."

"Oh, no," his friend assured him, "I had to get up to answer the phone anyhow."

"Henry, you are drunk," said his wife as they waited for the parking-lot attendant to bring them their car. "Don't you know why they say, 'Don't drink when you drive'?"

"I sure do," said Henry. "You might hit a bump and spill some."

A pink elephant, a green monkey, and a purple snake walked into a bar on the East Side.

The bartender looked up at the wild trio and said, "You guys are a little early tonight. He ain't here yet."

A drunk was up before the judge.

"The arresting officer claims you were drunk and disorderly. How do you plead?"

"Guilty, your honor," replied the drunk.

"Have you an explanation for your condition?" asked the judge.

"Well, your honor, I had these three purple snakes following me around all night, so I took a couple of drinks just to calm my nerves."

—●—

A cop stopped a drunk and told him to get into the patrol car. The drunk ignored the cop and kept on walking. The officer caught up with him and repeated the request. Still no reaction.

"Hey, Mac," said the cop. "Do you know who I am?"

"Can't say as I do," replied the drunk. "But if you tell me where you live, I'll be glad to drive you home."

—●—

A man helped his inebriated friend outside to get a breath of air.

"What time is it?" asked the drunk.

"One in the morning," replied his friend.

"I better go home or my wife will murder me. Where's my car?"

"You're in no condition to drive," said his friend. "Why don't you take a streetcar home?"

"Wouldn't do any good," said the drunk with a sigh. "My wife wouldn't let me keep it."

—●—

A drunk was walking down the street with one foot on the sidewalk and the other in the gutter when a cop stopped him and said, "Okay, buddy, let's go down to the station for a sobriety test."

The drunk looked the policeman right in the eye and declared, "You must be mistaken, officer. I haven't had a drink all evening."

"Is that so?" replied the cop. "Then maybe you'll tell me why you were walking down the street with one foot on the sidewalk and the other in the gutter."

The drunk thought for a moment and then replied, "Thank God you caught me, officer. I thought I was lame."

—●—

There's only one advantage to being a plain ordinary drunk instead of an alcoholic. If you're a drunk, you don't have to go to all those damned meetings.

—●—

The neighborhood priest was always trying to get Kelly to reform, but the old drunk would have none of it. One day the priest and Kelly were having a chat.

"Tell me, Father," said Kelly, "what is sciatica?"

The priest seized the opportunity to throw a scare into Kelly. "Sciatica is a very painful affliction usually caused by too much drink and a self-indulgent life."

"Is that so?" mused Kelly.

"Why do you ask?" said the priest.

"I was just wondering," replied Kelly. "I was just reading in the papers that the bishop is going back into the hospital. It seems he suffers from chronic sciatica."

—•—

Every night old Burt got drunk, and every night he came home with a wild story, which his wife failed to believe. One morning, around 2 A.M., Burt came home with a new approach.

"Honey," he said, "it was terrible. I was on my way down to the lobby when the elevator cable snapped, and we fell fifteen floors before we stopped. It was a miracle that I wasn't killed. But you can see how a man who had been through something like that would have to stop off for a drink to steady his nerves, now can't you, dear?"

This lengthy conversation had awakened Burt's son, and little Burt drank in every word. Before his wife could answer, his son interjected, "Gee, Pop, did you see the sins of your life flash before you just like people say you do?"

"Don't be ridiculous," snapped his mother. "Even if it is true, which I doubt, your father fell only fifteen floors."

—•—

A man stepped up to the bar and asked the bartender to mix him a very dry martini.

"Make it on a ratio of sixty to one," he said.

The bartender, being used to all kinds, simply said, "Okay, mister. Do you want a twist of lemon in it?"

"If I want lemonade, I'll order lemonade" was the emphatic reply.

—•—

Two firemen risked their lives to save a drunk from a hotel fire. His bed was in flames when they found him, and one of the firemen demanded, "Don't you know better than to smoke in bed? You could have burned up the whole hotel."

The drunk looked sheepish and replied, "Honest, mister, I wasn't smoking in bed. The bed was on fire when I got in."

— • —

Two men were discussing their actions when they got drunk.

"You know," said the first, "after a few drinks I have no trouble falling asleep. As a matter of fact, I'm asleep as soon as I hit the old bed."

"Oh," said his friend, "I don't have any trouble falling asleep either. My trouble after a few drinks is *hitting* the old bed."

— • —

Two drunks accidentally wandered into an amusement park and boarded a roller coaster. The ride was fast and furious, but it didn't seem to make much of an impression. As they were getting off, one drunk was heard to say, "You know, we may have made good time, but I have a feeling we took the wrong bus."

— • —

Two guys were having a friendly drink at their local bar. One drink led to another, and before long they were engaged in an old-fashioned drunk. They matched each other drink for drink until the wee hours of the morning. Finally one of the men lifted his glass, tossed down his drink, and fell over like an axed oak.

"You know, Sam," said his friend admiringly, "that's what I like about you. You know when to quit."

— • —

Two drunks were sitting in a local tavern one night when one said, "You know, Harry, this is just terrible. Night after night you and I meet, we go to the same bar, we sit in the same two seats, and we order the same drinks until we're too drunk to do anything but stagger home and fall into bed. I feel like my whole life is slipping away from me. What do you say that tonight we go out and find us a couple of girls and really do the town?"

"Naw," replied Harry, thinking wearily of his long-suffering wife, "I've got all the women I can handle waiting for me every night when I stagger home."

"Well, then," replied his friend, "let's buy a bottle and go up to your place."

—●—

Harry staggered in at 3 A.M. one morning to find his long-suffering wife waiting at the door.

"How can you come home like this?" she demanded. "You're half loaded!"

"It's very simple, my dear," slurred Harry. "I came home half loaded because I ran out of money."

—●—

A lady got on a bus and sat next to a man who was rather inebriated. He opened a paper bag he was holding on his lap and took out a bunch of grapes. He then opened the window and started throwing the grapes out the window, one at a time. She watched him for a minute or two and then asked him what he thought he was doing.

"I do this every time I take this bus," he replied unsteadily. "It keeps the elephants from attacking."

"But," she replied, "I don't see any elephants."

"Works every time" was his satisfied reply.

—●—

A very drunk man staggered up to a woman at a party and informed her that she was the ugliest woman he had ever seen. Holding her temper, the woman informed him that he was the drunkest man she had ever seen.

"That may be so," he replied, "but at least I'll be *sober* tomorrow morning."

—●—

A drunk stopped an elderly lady on the street and asked if she could direct him to the nearest branch of Alcoholics Anonymous. The lady was taken by the poor man's plight, and so she looked up the address for him and went so far as to offer to take him there herself so he could join.

"Join, hell!" he replied. "I want to resign."

—●—

The neighborhood drunk was hit by a car just as he was crossing the street to enter his favorite tavern. The bartender saw the accident and quickly called an ambulance. The rescue squad arrived, and one of the medics gave the injured man some medication.

Meanwhile another of the tavern's regulars was heard to say to the bartender, "I sure hope old Mac will be all right."

"He'll be up and around in a couple of days," said the bartender.

"What makes you think so?"

"Just look at him. He's trying to blow the foam off his medicine."

Two ladies found a man lying on the pavement one evening. Thinking to be of some assistance, they checked to see if he had some identification which might give them a clue to his trouble. They checked his wallet and his pockets but to no avail. Finally one of the ladies started tugging on a gold chain around his neck. Sure enough, there was a metal tag on the end which read, "If you read this while I am unconscious, do not give me any medication. I am a drunk."

A couple of student protesters were trying to set fire to the Washington Monument when a drunk wandered by. He looked carefully at the fire spreading around the base of the monument and then shook his head. "You'll never get it off the ground."

Two drunks were listening to a lecturer one night at the local soup kitchen. "You know who lives in the fanciest house in town?" demanded the lecturer. "The saloon-keeper, that's who! And who drives the best car in town? The saloon-keeper, that's who! And who runs around with all the loose women in town? The saloon-keeper, that's who! And who pays the bills for him? You poor, unfortunate drunks, that's who."

After the lecture was over, the temperance agent came over and sat down with the two drunks. "I certainly hope you two have seen the light," he said.

"We certainly have," admitted the drunks. "As a matter of fact, we are going to get a couple of jobs tomorrow morning and save our money and go into business."

"Why, that's just fine," beamed the temperance agent. "What kind of a business are you going to go into?"

"We're going to buy a saloon."

DUMBNESS

A group of tourists were taking a guided tour of a battleship.

The guide paused for a moment, pointed to a plaque set in the deck, and said dramatically, "This is where the captain fell."

"Well, young man, I can certainly see why," said a motherly little lady in the group, "I nearly tripped over it myself."

—●—

A brilliant archaeologist grew weary of spending his life among relics and ruins and decided to spend an evening on the town. He stopped in at a bar on the East Side and soon found himself talking to a beautiful girl. It didn't take him long to realize that she was none too bright, but what did it matter?

They left the bar and went to dinner and then on to a nightclub. The archaeologist grew daring and whispered that he would like nothing better than to take her back to his apartment and show her his private collection of dinosaur bones. Much to his happy surprise, she agreed.

They went back to his apartment, and he began showing her the treasures he had collected over the years. As she browsed through them, she suddenly pointed to one object and asked in a shocked tone, "What's that?"

"Oh," replied the professor, "that's a phallic symbol. It's used by native tribes in their fertility rites."

"Well," she replied, much relieved, "I'd hate to tell you what it *looks* like."

—●—

"My Uncle Harry was so dumb," said one convict to another while comparing family trees, "that he telephoned a bank clerk, told him that it was a stickup, and then told the clerk to mail him ten thousand dollars."

—●—

Two neighbors were chatting. "I hear Mrs. Latimer just had triplets," said the first.

"Really? I understand that that happens only once in every fifteen thousand times," said her friend.

"No wonder she never finds any time to do her housework."

—•—

A young lady was having quite a problem with her boyfriend. Whereas most girls have trouble keeping men from getting too familiar, she was having trouble getting him to do much more than hold her hand.

Finally, aggravated beyond endurance by his lack of aggressiveness, she demanded, "How would you like to see where I was operated on for appendicitis?"

"Gee," he stammered, "I'd really rather not. I've always hated hospitals."

—•—

Two show girls bumped into each other in the ladies' room of a fashionable resort hotel.

Thinking to impress the other ladies in the room, the first show girl said, "I'm sure we've met before in Cannes."

"Oh, really," replied the second show girl. "This one or the one at the Fontainebleau?"

—•—

"John, I think we're going to have to fire that new cook."

"Why, dear? It took us so long to find her."

"Yes, but she's so slow. This morning I asked her to dice some potatoes, and she still isn't finished. It shouldn't take that long to dice potatoes."

"Did you see what's taking her so long?"

"She's drawing little black dots on them."

EDUCATION

"Teacher," said young Bill, "do you believe that people should be punished for things they haven't done?"

"Of course not."

"I'm glad to hear that because I haven't done my homework."

—•—

"But Professor Quimbly, I really did my best on this exam," said the earnest young student. "I really don't think I deserve a zero."

"Neither do I, my boy," agreed the prof, "but it's the lowest grade I'm permitted to give."

—●—

At a progressive school in New York children are being taught foreign languages in kindergarten. Some teachers sometimes wonder if the students aren't even more progressive than the schools they attend. One teacher asked six-year-old Wendy if she knew the difference between "madame" and "mademoiselle." Little Wendy knew very well. " 'Monsieur' is the difference" came the child's irrefutable reply.

ELEPHANTS

An elephant escaped from the local zoo and made his way into the vegetable garden of one of the town's most prominent matrons. Unfortunately this lady had only just returned from a cocktail party where she had had just a little too much to drink. She was not too drunk, however, to see the beast in her garden, and she had the presence of mind to call the police.

"Quick," she said, "there's some kind of huge, strange-looking animal in my garden."

"What's he doing?" asked the desk sergeant.

"He seems to be picking lettuce with his tail."

"Oh, really?" replied the wary policeman. "And what's he doing with it?"

The lady peered out into her garden once more and then said, "Sergeant, even if I told you, you'd never believe it."

—●—

A man rushed up to a policeman yelling, "Help! Help! I've been robbed."

"Take it easy, Mac," replied the policeman, taking out his notebook. "Tell me, what did the guy look like?"

"What guy?"

"The guy who robbed you. Give me a description."

"There wasn't any guy. I was robbed by an elephant."

"Okay," said the cop. "Then give me a description of the elephant."

"Are you kidding? It was an elephant. A big gray elephant with four legs and a trunk."

"Don't get touchy, Mac," said the cop. "Elephants have characteristics which identify them. For instance, if the elephant that robbed you had big ears, he was an African elephant. If he had smaller ears, he was an Asian elephant. So which was he—African or Asian?"

"How should I know?" cried the distressed victim. "He had a stocking pulled down over his face."

EQUALITY

Anybody who insists that all men are created equal obviously never took a shower in the army.

ESKIMOS

"Tell me, class, what do you know about Eskimos?" asked the teacher.

Young Mike's hand shot up. "I know all about Eskimos," he bragged. "They're in the Bible. They're God's frozen people."

ETIQUETTE

Little Bobby always looked to his older brother for explanations of things he didn't quite understand. One day the two boys were sitting in the backyard, staying out of the way while their mother entertained her bridge club. Bobby was always a bit puzzled by the fuss his mother made over her bridge club, since they were the same ladies she saw every day in the supermarket, the laundry, the schoolyard, and the P.T.A. He once asked her about it, but she had only said something he didn't quite understand about "etiquette." And so he took the matter up with his brother.

"Hey," said little Bobby, "what's etiquette?"

"Oh, you know," replied his brother with great assurance. "It's like yawning only with your mouth *closed*."

—•—

After much prompting from her mother, little Abigail, the most notorious tomboy in the neighborhood, wrote this thank-you note to her grandmother: "Dear Granny, thank you so much for the birthday present you sent me. I always wanted a sewing box, even though I never wanted one very much."

FAIR PLAY

A loving couple was startled by a noise in the corridor. The woman got up and cautiously opened the door just far enough to peek out. She returned to the living room looking greatly relieved.

"Relax, darling," she said. "It was just my husband sneaking into *your* apartment."

FAITH HEALERS

Two ladies were sitting in the doctor's office comparing notes.

"I don't know what to do," said the first woman sadly. "I just hope this doctor can help me. My husband and I want a baby more than anything else. We've tried just about everything, but nothing seems to work."

"I know just how you feel," said the second woman sympathetically. "I had the same problem, but now I'm going to have a baby next fall."

"Oh, that's wonderful," said the first woman. "What did you do?"

"I went to a faith healer."

"Oh," said the first woman. "My husband and I went to one for nearly a year. It didn't do any good."

The other woman smiled and said softly, "Take my advice, my dear. Go alone."

FATHERS

"You know," said Elvira to her father, "my fiancé says he was born with a silver spoon in his mouth."

"That may be," replied her dad, "but I'd bet a hundred bucks it had somebody else's initials on it."

—●—

"Dad, I think I'm in love with this girl. . . ."

"That's wonderful, son," said his relieved parent as he glanced over his son's shoulder-length hair, flowered shirt, and beaded necklace. "Thank God, you've made the right choice."

—●—

Irate father bursting into the darkened living room: "I'll teach you to kiss my daughter."

"It's too late, sir," replied the young man. "I already know how."

—•—

A beautiful young girl went into a card shop. She looked around for several minutes but couldn't seem to find what she wanted.

The clerk stepped up and inquired, "May I help you, miss?"

"I hope so," she replied. "Do you have any Father's Day cards that begin 'To whom it may concern'?"

FAUX PAS

A young lady struck up a conversation with a gentleman at the country club. He asked her to dance, and while they moved around the floor, her eye came to rest on another man leaning against the wall.

"Good grief!" she exclaimed, "what a homely man."

Her partner replied in a rather strained voice, "That man is my brother."

"Oh, I'm so sorry," she cried, "but at first I didn't notice any resemblance."

FEET

Maybelle was out for a stroll in the park when she came across her friend Alice sitting on a bench with her shoes off.

"What's the matter, Alice?"

"I've got corns."

"Well, why don't you do something for them?" asked Maybelle.

"Why should I?" snapped Alice. "What have they ever done for me?"

FIREMEN

A fireman risked his life to save a beautiful young girl. As he carried her half-naked body from the burning building she whispered, "You're so brave. It must have taken a great deal of courage to rescue me."

"It sure did," admitted the noble fireman. "First I had to fight three other guys who wanted to save you."

FISH STORIES

"Jake, it's getting late, and we haven't caught a thing. What do you say we call it a day and go home?"

"But, Harry, it's still early! Let's let at least two more big ones get away before we give up."

—●—

Mr. Adam's fishing trip was hardly what you might call a success—four days at the lake and not a single fish. On his way back home he stopped in at the local fish market and astonished the clerk with this request.

"Hey, buddy, throw me four trout, will you?"

Thinking he might not have heard the man correctly, the clerk hesitated and looked questioningly at the frustrated fisherman.

Mr. Adams sensed the clerk's reluctance to throw four fish at a customer, so he explained the situation. "Look, buddy, I may not be much of a fisherman, but if I take home four trout, I want to be able to tell my wife I *caught* them."

FISHING

"Mr. Wingate," said the minister with a frown, "I know perfectly well you didn't come to church this Sunday so you could play nine holes of golf."

"That's a lie," said Mr. Wingate, "and I've got the fish to prove it."

—●—

After catching her husband sneaking out of the house one morning at 5 A.M., Agnes demanded, "Why didn't you tell me you wanted to go fishing?"

"Simple, my dear. Because I want to *go* fishing."

FLATTERY

Two old men found themselves sharing a cell in the county jail.

"What are you in for?" asked one old man.

"Well, about six weeks ago I was standing in front of a tavern when this gorgeous young girl came rushing up to me dragging a policeman. She took one look at me and started yelling, 'That's him, officer. He's the one. He's the man who attacked me.' "

"Were you the one?" asked his cellmate.

"Heck, no," replied the old-timer. "But I was so flattered I admitted it."

FLIRT

A pretty young girl drove straight through a red light only to have a patrol officer blow the whistle at her. Paying him no heed, she continued on her way. The cop leaped on his motorcycle and finally caught up with her three blocks away.

"What's the matter, lady," he demanded, "didn't you hear me whistle?"

"Certainly," she replied with a smile, "but I never flirt when I'm driving."

THE FLOOD

A traveling salesman found himself stranded in a very small town due to a heavy rainstorm which had washed out the road he normally took out of town. While having a cup of coffee in the hotel dining room, he looked out the window and remarked to the waitress, "Did you ever see such rain? It looks like the Flood."

"It looks like the *what*, mister?"

"The Flood. Surely you have read about the Flood and how Noah finally landed the Ark safely on Mount Ararat."

"Can't say as I have," replied the waitress. "But then I ain't seen a paper in a month."

FOOTBALL

"Why is a lousy football team like counterfeit money?"

"Because the halves are full of lead, and the quarters can't pass."

—•—

A big university in the South is going to have three football squads next year. One squad is going to play offense. One is going to play defense. The third is going to attend classes.

—•—

A couple of reporters were interviewing the coach of a local football team.

"Tell me, coach," said the first reporter, "do you think all young men should play football?"

"I certainly do," said the coach. "Football helps a man develop individuality, initiative, and leadership."

"Tell me," said the second reporter, "how do you get along with the men on your team?"

"Fine," replied the coach, "just fine as long as they do exactly what I tell them."

FOUR-LETTER WORDS

Kids are awfully smart these days, but sometimes I wonder about their parents. I heard one mother giving her son a lecture about using four-letter words.

"But, Mom," protested the boy, "Norman Mailer uses words like that all the time."

"Well," replied his mother, "if that's where you're getting it, I don't want you to play with him anymore."

—•—

"I think it's terrible the way women talk today," confided a notorious playboy to a talk-show host. "They just ruin their feminine appeal when they use all those four-letter words."

"What words?" inquired the host. "Oh, you know. Words like 'can't' and 'won't' and 'don't.' "

—•—

Little Sammy, much to his mother's horror, got into the habit of using very bad words. Time after time she punished him, and time after time he promised never to do it again. But just as soon as he got excited some awful word or phrase slipped out. Finally, in desperation, his mother packed some of his belongings in a suitcase and put it in the front hall. "Now, I'm warning you," she said, "one more bad word, and out you go." She was sure that this final threat would cure him, and for a few days it did, but one afternoon while he was playing with some friends, he forgot and in his excitement let loose a stream of language that chilled his mother's heart. She marched to the front hall, picked up his suitcase, and as he was trying to enter the house, handed it to him and told him to be on his way. About fifteen minutes later she stuck her head out the front door to see what was up. There sat little Sammy, tears streaming down his cheeks.

"Well," she demanded sternly, "why haven't you gone?"

"Because," sobbed her son, "I don't know where the hell to go."

FREE LOVE

Husband to tired-looking wife: "Honey, do you believe in free love?"

"Have I ever sent you a bill?" was her weary reply.

THE FRENCH

Three young French boys were spending the summer in the country. One afternoon they were strolling through a field when they happened to see a couple lying under a tree, locked in a loving embrace.

"Mon Dieu," exclaimed the youngest boy, who was only six, "those people are having a terrible fight."

"But no, mon petit," replied the more sophisticated nine-year-old. "Those people are making love."

"True," agreed the oldest boy, a lad of eleven years. "But what amateurs."

—●—

The wise old Frenchman and his grandson were having a glass of wine together in a little sidewalk café.

"Tell me, Grandfather," said the young man, "do you think I should talk to my wife when I make love?"

"Mais oui!" cried his grandfather, "if you happen to be near a telephone."

—●—

A very wealthy and sophisticated Frenchman was known for his savoir-faire. Take his wife's funeral, for example. He stood stoically through the services and showed very little emotion as the casket was lowered to its final resting place. However, after the funeral he went over and comforted the young man everyone knew to be his wife's lover.

"Ah, mon ami," he said as he placed an arm comfortingly around the distraught young man. "Do not take it too badly. After all, I may marry again."

FRIENDSHIP

Two women were having lunch a few days after Thanksgiving.

"Well," said the first, "Christmas is just around the corner. I guess I'd better get started on my Christmas shopping. Shall we meet in town next week?"

"Not me," replied her friend. "I bought all my Christmas presents last September."

"Really," said the first. "Tell me, how did you know way back then who your friends were going to be in December?"

—•—

The Lone Ranger and Tonto were trapped in a wagon, surrounded by hostile Indians. It looked like the end for the brave pair.

"It looks like this is it, Tonto. I think we're done for," said the Lone Ranger.

"What do you mean 'we,' paleface?"

—•—

"I had a wonderful dream last night," said one young fellow to his friend. "I dreamed I was in Monte Carlo gambling, and I just couldn't lose. I won every pot. It was the best dream I've ever had."

"I had a wonderful dream last night myself," said his friend. "I was all alone in my apartment when the doorbell rang and these two gorgeous blondes walked in. The two of them spent the night with me drinking, dancing, and making love to me."

"Some friend," said the first young man. "Why didn't you call me?"

"I did," his friend assured him. "But you were in Monte Carlo."

FRUIT

A couple of fruit-growers met at a convention and started bragging about the size of the fruit grown in their respective states.

The man from Florida picked up a melon and said, "Is this the biggest apple you people can grow out here?"

"Please," snapped the Californian, "don't squeeze the grapes."

GARDENERS

Mrs. Van Farkle was the town's wealthiest resident. She was also the president of the local ladies' garden club. Flowers were her greatest interest. So it was only natural when her trusted gardener had an attack of appendicitis that she would visit him in the hospital. She arrived at the hospital after visiting hours were officially over, but the nurse at the desk seemed helpful.

"I guess we can make an exception," said the nurse. "Are you his wife?"

"Certainly not, my dear," replied the wealthy matron. "*I* am his mistress."

GAS

A little red sports car drifted to a stop high on a deserted mountain road.

"Sorry, baby," said the driver with an evil grin, "it looks like we're out of gas."

"Funny," replied his lovely companion as she opened her bag and took out a giant-sized flask, "I had a feeling this might happen."

"Well, what do you know?" said her date, eyeing the flask. "You really are a swinger after all. What did you bring? Scotch or bourbon?"

"Gasoline," she replied with a smile.

GENERATION GAP

During one "generation gap" quarrel with his parents young Michael cried, "I want excitement, adventure, money, and beautiful women. I'll never find it here at home, so I'm leaving. Don't try and stop me!"

With that he headed toward the door. His father rose and followed close behind.

"Didn't you hear what I said? I don't want you to try and stop me."

"Who's trying to stop you?" replied his father. "If you wait a minute, I'll go with you."

—●—

"I'm surprised at you, child!" scolded Cindy's grandmother. "When I was your age, a nice girl didn't even hold a man's hand."

"But, Grandma," replied Cindy, "today a nice girl *has* to hold a man's hand."

—●—

"Tell me," said the young reporter, "do you think that the younger generation is on the road to ruin?"

"I sure do, sonny," replied the octogenarian. "I've thought so for the last sixty years."

—●—

Mr. and Mrs. Levine worked their fingers to the bone just so that their son, Sam, could go to college and become a doctor. When he was accepted at a very fancy college, they were overjoyed, and they spared no expense to send him off in style. A few months later he returned for Thanksgiving vacation, and the Levines went to the airport to meet him.

When he got off the plane, Mrs. Levine threw her arms around him and cried, "Samela, it's so good to have you home."

Her son drew back and said, "Please, Mother, you must stop calling me Samela. I'm eighteen years old now, not a little boy."

His mother apologized meekly and tried a new topic of conversation. "Were you a good boy? Did you eat only kosher, like I told you?"

But again Samuel was firm. "Mother, this is the twentieth century," he said. "It's foolish to observe all those old dietary laws when everyone knows they were invented only because of dangers to your health. All of those dangers are gone now that we have refrigeration and chemical preservatives. I don't keep kosher, and you shouldn't bother to, either."

"Well," said his mother, "did you at least go to synagogue?"

"To tell the truth, Mother, I didn't. All the guys go to the college chapel on Sunday for a nondenominational service."

At this point Mrs. Levine lost control. "Just tell me one thing, Samuel," she said bitterly. "Are you still circumcized?"

GENEROSITY

Talk about being generous. Why, I knew a guy who was so generous with his girl friend that he finally had to marry her for *his* money.

GIFTS

A man from a very poor family finally made his fortune. He owned a huge chain of hardware stores, and the money just poured in. He wanted to do something special for his mother, since she was the one who encouraged him and kept telling him that she knew he would make it. He searched far and wide for the gift that would make her happy. Finally he found it: a parrot who could recite all the Psalms. It was perfect for his devoted mother, although it was very expensive: $25,000. Nothing was too good for his mother, however, so he bought the bird and had it shipped directly to her. He waited nearly a week, but not a word of thanks did he hear. Finally he called his mother.

"Mom," he said, "did you get my present?"

"I sure did, son," she replied. "And he was delicious."

—•—

"I want to buy a gift for my rich old uncle," said the customer. "The poor old man can hardly get around at all. His eyesight is bad, his hands shake, and his legs aren't steady. Have you any suggestions?"

"Well," replied the clerk thoughtfully, "you might give some thought to a nice can of floor wax."

GOLD DIGGERS

"Daddy," said little John, "Mommy says your new secretary looks like a gold digger. What's a 'gold digger'?"

"Well," replied his dad, "a gold digger is a woman who's got what it takes to take what you've got."

GOLF

"I want you to know that this is not the game I usually play," snapped an irate golfer to his caddy.

"I should hope not, sir. So tell me," inquired the caddy, "what game *do* you usually play?"

—•—

A golfer was having a fight with his wife. He finally had enough and yelled, "Shut up, or you'll drive me out of my mind."

"That wouldn't be a drive," snapped his wife. "That would be a putt."

—•—

A man was about to tee off when he noticed a funeral procession driving through the golf course. As it passed by, one of the members of his foursome took off his hat and wiped a tear from his eye.

"How odd!" said one player. "I've never seen a funeral procession on a golf course before, but it certainly was very respectful of you to take off your hat."

"Oh, it's little enough I could do. She and I would have celebrated our twentieth anniversary next week."

—•—

A minister joined two members of his congregation and the local golf pro for eighteen holes on Saturday afternoon. The minister's game was way off that day, and the pro was anything but sympathetic. He spent most of the afternoon sneering at what he called the minister's ungodly game.

Back in the clubhouse the pro didn't let up. He regaled the other members with stories of the minister's every blunder, and as a parting shot he sneered, "Let's do it again, preacher. If you can find anybody else to make it a foursome, I'd be glad to play you again."

"We might have a game next Saturday," replied the minister. "I doubt if any of my friends can play, but why don't you invite your parents? After the game I could even marry them for you."

—•—

Overheard on the links:
Golfer: "You have got to be the world's worst caddy!"
Caddy: "Well, how's that for coincidence?"

GOSSIP

A man was cornered by the local gossip, who took the opportunity to go on at great length about town scandals, some of which were forty years old. Finally he managed to get a word in and told her that he had to leave.

"Oh," she said, "I hope I haven't encroached too much upon your time."

"Madam," he replied, "you have been trespassing on eternity."

GOVERNMENT SPENDING

An eager young book salesman approached an old Tennessee farmer with the idea of selling him a set of books on the science of agriculture.

"Now, tell me, boy," drawled the farmer, "what would I want with a set of books like that?"

"Why, if you had these books, you could farm twice as good as you do now," replied the salesman.

"Son," drawled the old farmer, "as it is, with what the government pays me not to plant I don't farm half as good as I know how."

—●—

You know, it's sad. In the good, old days America was the land of milk and honey. Every man had his chance to become a millionaire. Think of the fortunes that have been thrown away on drinking, gambling, and beautiful women. But that's all over now. After all, we have a *government* to support.

—●—

All the big cities are in trouble. One mayor has even proposed that his city become the fifty-first state. Personally I think he'd do better if his city seceded from the Union completely. Then he could apply for foreign aid.

GROUP THERAPY

I don't go to an analyst anymore. I'm in group therapy now. Actually, it's the same thing—only they use bunk beds.

GUESTS

A rather inebriated guest drew his host aside and inquired if he and one of the female guests might borrow the guest bedroom.

"Be my guest," replied the host. "But what about your wife?"

"Don't worry," the guest assured him. "With so many people here she won't even notice I'm gone."

"Oh," replied the host, "I'm afraid she won't be able to help but notice. You see, she and my brother-in-law just borrowed the guest bedroom."

HARD-LUCK STORIES

Two men were exchanging hard-luck stories.

"You think you've had tough luck?" said one. "Why, I had everything a man could want: a good job, a beautiful apartment, a foreign sports car, and the most gorgeous redhead you've ever seen. I really had it made until my *wife* found out."

—•—

Two bums came to rest on the same park bench and struck up a conversation. Eventually they got around to how each of them had come to such dire straits.

One explained, "You are looking at a man who never took a word of advice from any man!"

"Isn't that a coincidence?" replied the other. "You are looking at a man who took everybody's advice."

—•—

Two deadbeats were comparing hard-luck stories. The first told a sad tale of bankruptcy, divorce, drunkenness, and dissolution.

"I don't think," he sighed, "that I have ever done anything right in my whole life."

"Listen, Mac," said his companion, "you think you're a failure? Why, when I told my son about the birds and the bees, I made such a mess of it that a few weeks later I caught him at the drive-in with a woodpecker and a hornet."

—•—

"Did you hear about poor Charlie?" asked one hood of another.

"No, what happened?"

"Poor guy. He scrimped and saved for years just to get the money to buy his poor old mother a house. And he finally made it. Poor woman wasn't open a week when the cops arrested her for running it."

HAREM

Did you hear what happened to the Arab who arrived home a day early? Well, it seems that while he was going in the front door of the harem, his wives let out a terrific sheik.

HEAVEN

Mrs. O'Hara, a widow of some five years, went to visit a famous medium, thinking she might contact her late husband, Mike. The medium assured her that every effort would be made and that they would hold a séance that very evening. Several believers gathered around the table, and the medium ordered that the lights be dimmed and that everyone at the table join hands. A hush fell over the room, and the medium called the name Mike O'Hara over and over again.

Suddenly a strange calm seemed to permeate the room, and a distant voice, faint at first but growing stronger and stronger, cried, "I am Mike O'Hara. Who is it who calls my spirit forth?"

The medium replied that it was indeed his own wife who called upon him and that Mrs. O'Hara wished to speak to him. The spirit replied that he would speak to his wife.

"Mike," said Mrs. O'Hara, "are you all right?"

"Yes," he replied, "I am all right."

"Tell me, are you happy there?"

"Yes, I am happy here."

"Are you happier there than you were on earth with me?"

"Yes," replied the spirit, "I am much happier here than I was on earth with you."

Mrs. O'Hara seemed a bit shaken, but she had one last question. "Tell me, my husband, what is it like there? What is heaven really like?"

"Don't be absurd, woman," roared the truthful spirit. "Whatever made you think I was in *heaven?*"

HIPPIES

A hippie was strolling down the Sunset Strip with a live pig tucked underneath his arm. Two of his buddies who were in the neighborhood met him on the corner.

"Hey, man," said one of his friends, "where did you get *him?*"

The pig looked up and said, "I bought him at an auction."

—●—

Two hippies were walking down the street.

"You know, man," said one, "I'm really worried."

"What's the problem?" his friend inquired.

"Well, last night I was talking to my parents, and I'm beginning to see my old man's point of view."

—●—

A hippie chugged up to a toll gate in a beat-up, broken-down jalopy.

"Fifty cents," said the toll-keeper.

"Sold, man, sold," cried the hippie.

HOLLYWOOD

A producer spotted a lovely blonde at a recent Hollywood cocktail party and zeroed in on her.

"I'd just love to take an experienced girl like you home this evening," he said with a lecherous grin.

"I am not an experienced girl," she replied in a chilly tone.

"You aren't home yet, either, honey," he replied.

—●—

Money is tight in Hollywood these days. A character actor wanted a thousand dollars to play an Indian in a TV Western. His agent called to tell him he would be getting five hundred for the job. When he protested, his agent informed him that it was only fair. They couldn't afford a thousand for an Indian, so they rewrote his part. He was now going to play a half-breed.

—●—

A leading Beverly Hills psychiatrist has been giving nearly all of his attention to one patient. One evening he and a colleague happened to be discussing the case.

"My patient is in a terrible mental state," admitted the physician.

"What seems to be the cause of her acute depression?" asked his friend.

"She's terribly upset by the fact that she can't sing, she can't dance, she can't play a musical instrument, and worst of all, that she couldn't act her way out of a paper bag."

"I take it," said his colleague, "that these accomplishments which she lacks tend to frustrate some childhood ambition and therefore cause her depression?"

"Not at all, Doctor," replied the lady's physician. "Her depression is due to feelings of anxiety and fear. You see, my friend, she is a big star."

—●—

It was Henry's first experience at a wild Hollywood party. He wandered through the orgy amazed at what he saw going on around him. Finally he noticed a very pretty girl sitting very quietly in a corner watching the goings-on around her with what seemed to be a great deal of disdain. Henry made his way across the room and introduced himself.

"I'm afraid that you and I just don't fit in with a bunch of swingers like this. Why don't you let me take you home?"

"That would be fine," replied the girl with a shy smile. "Where do you live?"

—●—

An agent I know called me a couple of weeks ago. When I asked him how things were going, he told me a very sad story. It seems he has a client with a figure like Sophia Loren, who sings like Judy Garland, and on top of that is a graduate of a very fine dramatic school. I couldn't understand his problem. I told him a girl with that combination of looks and talent would be a star in no time. Then he told me the sad part. His client is a *boy*.

HONESTY

After watching the delivery boy stagger up four flights of stairs laden with parcels from the supermarket, the lady of the house inquired, "Does the market allow you to accept tips?"

"No, ma'am" was his reply. "But if they asked me if you gave me one, I'd lie like crazy to save you."

—●—

A father was looking over his son's report card. "Well, I'll say one thing for you. With grades as bad as these you must be the most honest boy in your class. You couldn't possibly be cheating."

—●—

A little boy rushed into the house to show his father the brand-new penknife he had found.

"That's a fine knife, son, but are you *sure* it was lost?"

"Of course, I'm sure," replied his honest offspring. "I even saw the guy who was looking for it."

—•—

"I'm going to fire that laundress," snarled Mrs. Fischer. "She stole two of my towels."

"Which towels did she steal?" inquired Mr. Fischer.

"The ones we got from that hotel in Las Vegas."

HORSES

Returning from his first horseback ride, six-year-old Kevin was overheard to say, "I never thought anything stuffed with hay could be so hard."

—•—

"Why, this horse is so smart," bragged the farmer, "he knows as much as I do."

"Now, you just hush up," snapped his wife. "You may want to sell that horse someday."

—•—

"Hey, Harry, hear you went to the track the other day. How did you make out?"

"Are you kidding? The nag I bet on took so long to cross the finish line the jockey should have packed a change of saddle."

—•—

A guy went to the track and won three hundred dollars. Thinking his luck would hold, he went back the next day ready to make a killing. As he was looking over the horses set to run in the last race, he noticed a priest making signs over one of the nags. Thinking that he had really lucked in, the guy bet every nickel he had won and every cent he could scrape up on the horse. Naturally the horse finished last. Leaving the track, he happened to bump into the very priest he had seen blessing the horse.

"Father," he said, "I'm a ruined man. I saw you blessing that horse, and I bet every cent I had on him."

The priest was horrified. "My son," he said, "I was not blessing that horse; I was administering the last rites."

HOTELS

The house detective began getting complaints from the neighbors on both sides of Room 1523. He checked the register and found that the room was rented to a Miss Cordelia Witherspoon, a single lady from Massachusetts who had come to the hotel to attend a teachers' convention.

Thinking there must be some mistake and that the noise her neighbors were complaining about was coming from some other room, the detective picked up the phone, dialed Miss Witherspoon's number, and inquired discreetly, "Miss Witherspoon, are you entertaining?"

"Just a minute, honey" came Miss Witherspoon's reply. "Hold on while I ask him."

I've stayed in some pretty crummy hotels in my time, but the one I stayed in last night was so bad that I called room service and asked them to send me up a room.

A guest stopped in at the hotel manager's office and requested the name of the girl who operated the switchboard.

"We don't give out information of that kind," replied the manager stiffly.

"But I only want to send her some flowers."

"Why, sir, how kind!" exclaimed the manager. "I'm sure she will appreciate the thought."

"Appreciate it, hell!" snarled the guest. "I thought she was dead."

Desk clerk: "Would you like the switchboard operator to wake you in the morning?"

Guest: "That won't be necessary. I always seem to wake up around seven."

Desk clerk: "Really? Then, would you mind giving our operator a call?"

HOUSEKEEPER

She is really some housekeeper. She's been divorced five times, and she's kept the house every time.

INFLATION

With food prices soaring sometimes I think it would be cheaper to eat the money.

—●—

Last payday Jim Harmon received a blank check by mistake. He never reported it, and it took the paymaster two weeks to catch the error. He called Harmon into his office and asked him why he hadn't come to complain about not getting paid.

"Well," replied Harmon, "to tell you the truth I didn't think it was a mistake. With the way things are going I just thought my deductions had finally caught up with my salary."

IN-LAWS

"I wish I knew where Henry was," the new bride said with a sigh.

"I presume, my dear," hissed her mother-in-law, "that you wish you knew where Henry *is*."

"Not at all. Henry is upstairs in bed with a black eye and a terrible hangover. I know where he is; I just wish I knew where he was."

—●—

"So, my boy, you want to become my son-in-law," snarled old Bigelow.

"Well, not exactly," admitted young Jack, "but I want to marry your daughter, so I guess there's no other way."

—●—

"Young man," boomed the father of the bride-to-be, "are you prepared to support a family?"

"No, sir," replied the lad. "I figure on supporting your daughter. The rest of you will just have to shift for yourselves."

—●—

"John," said young Alice to her fiancé, "it isn't that mother doesn't like you. It's just that she thinks that you're effeminate."

"Well," mused John, "compared with her, I probably am."

—•—

A prominent businessman decided to go on a safari in Africa. It was, he thought, just the place to get away from it all. However, it wasn't long before his wife decided to tag along, and her mother decided that she would go, too. So the three of them wound up out in the jungle together. One morning the businessman and his wife got up and were halfway through breakfast before realizing that Mother was nowhere in sight. The two of them rushed out to search for her, and after an hour or so they came to a clearing. There she was, crouched behind a tree, and about twenty yards away was a huge lion. "Herbert!" shrieked his wife. "What shall we do?"

"Not a thing, my dear," replied Herbert. "If that lion was dumb enough to get into a fix like that, let *him* get himself out of it."

INSOMNIA

Mr. Ricter tried everything for his insomnia, but nothing seemed to help. Night after night he tossed and turned but never managed more than a few minutes' sleep. Doctor after doctor failed to find a cure, and the poor man became resigned to a life of sleepless nights. One evening he stopped in at a local tavern and slumped wearily against the bar.

The bartender listened sympathetically as the poor fellow spoke of night after sleepless night and finally said, "I think I know a way to put an end to this problem." Ricter was skeptical but at this point willing to try anything. "My uncle Harry couldn't sleep either," said the bartender, "but this is what did the trick. Go home and get ready for bed. If you can't sleep within fifteen minutes, get up, get a glass, put a lump of sugar in the bottom, cover the sugar with good bourbon, and drink it down. Then go back to bed. If you aren't asleep in fifteen minutes, get up and do it again. Then, if you still can't sleep, do it again. Keep on doing it and it will do for you what it did for Uncle Harry."

"You mean it really put him to sleep?"

"Well, not exactly," admitted the bartender. "But now he doesn't mind staying awake."

—•—

An old man, notorious for his laziness, visited his doctor and complained bitterly about his insomnia.

"Doc," he moaned, "you've just got to help me. I've got insomnia so bad I keep waking up nearly every three days."

—●—

A man spent thousands of dollars going from doctor to doctor trying to find a cure for his insomnia. Finally a doctor was able to help him.

"You must be terribly relieved," said one of his friends sympathetically.

"You said it," replied the former insomniac. "Why, sometimes I lie awake all night thinking of how I used to suffer."

INSURANCE

Two insurance agents were having a heated discussion concerning the speed with which their rival companies paid claims.

"Why, if you were to die today," said the first, "my company would have a check in your widow's hands by tomorrow morning."

"Well," replied the second, "you may be able to wait that long, but if you were to decide to jump off the roof of the building where my company's offices are located, we would have your check ready for you by the time you passed our floor on your way down."

—●—

A life-insurance company which prided itself on efficiency sent one of its agents out to see the widow Murphy the day after her husband's funeral. Judging everything to be in order, the agent produced a check for fifty thousand dollars and presented it to the widow. Mrs. Murphy was quite overcome, and it took several minutes before she could get hold of herself.

"You know," she sobbed, "Murphy was such a *good* husband. Why, I'd give fifteen thousand of this to have him back right now."

INTRODUCTIONS

A beautiful girl was ushered into the judge's chambers.

"Please, your honor," she pleaded, "I've just been introduced to a man, and we want to get married. We don't want to wait for three days. Can't you help us?"

Not wanting to stand in the way of true love, the judge waived the three-day waiting period and married the young couple himself. Less than a week later the same girl was back, this time pleading that the judge grant her a divorce.

"But why?" asked the judge. "You were so enthusiastic after just having been introduced."

"Well, your honor," she replied, "he was the most overintroduced man I've ever met."

—•—

A very pretty girl took her seat on a plane next to a good-looking air force captain. The young officer obviously admired his traveling companion, but being an officer and a gentleman he started off like this.

"Pardon me, miss, but do you know Captain Barrett, of the United States Air Force?"

"Why, no, I'm afraid I don't," she replied.

"Well, then," he said with a smile, "allow me to introduce myself."

THE IRISH

It was three in the morning when a loud knocking awakened Mrs. O'Malley from a deep sleep. She threw open the door, and the caller demanded, "Be you the widow O'Malley?"

"I'm Mrs. O'Malley," she replied firmly, "but I'm no widow. And you must be drunk to be waking me up at this time of night and asking me such questions."

"Don't be too quick to judge, lass" was the stranger's reply. "Wait until you see what the boys are carrying up the stairs."

THE ITALIANS

An irate Italian policeman was in the process of arresting an unruly and very drunk American tourist.

"It is my duty to inform you," said the carabiniere sternly, "that just as in your country, anything you say may be held against you."

"That's wonderful," said the drunken tourist. "How about 'Sophia Loren'?"

JETS

Two matrons boarded a jet bound for Miami. "You know, Sadie," said the first lady, "this plane travels faster than sound."

"You don't say!" replied Sadie. "I think that's terrible."

A stewardess happened to overhear Sadie's remark and inquired if there was anything wrong.

"Well," said Sadie, "it's just that my friend tells me that this plane will fly faster than sound."

"That's true," replied the stewardess, "but there really isn't anything to be afraid of."

"Oh," replied Sadie, "I'm not afraid. It's just that I wish you'd ask the captain to slow down. My friend and I might want to talk a little."

JEWS

An after-dinner speaker started telling a story by saying, "It seems there were two Jews . . ." when he was interrupted by a guest who demanded to know why stories had to begin like that.

"You're right," admitted the speaker sheepishly. "It isn't kind to keep telling stories about the Jews all the time. How about this one? It's the story of two Chinese gentlemen."

"Well, I guess that's better," admitted the somewhat mollified guest.

"It seems there were these two Chinamen who met on their way to the synagogue. . . ."

JOBS

"Calvin Woodbridge took a job at this fish cannery when he was fifteen years old," beamed the president to his assembled workers. "And today Cal is one hundred years old and still working at that same job." The workers roared their approval. "But," continued the speaker, "there comes a time in every man's life when he has done his work and earned his rest. So today I am going to retire old Cal and pay him half salary for life. What do you think of that, Cal?"

"I'll tell you what I think," snarled the old New Englander who had remained silent throughout the proceedings. "I think I'm going to sue this company for breach of promise."

"Why, whatever for?" gasped the president.

"Because when I took this job, sonny, your grandpa promised me it would be *permanent*."

—●—

While applying for a job, the pretty young applicant boasted that she was a prizewinner in several crossword-puzzle contests and had won first prize with her slogan for a local restaurant's radio advertising.

"That's all well and good," said her potential boss, "but we are looking for someone who can be that smart during office hours."

"Oh, yes," said the applicant earnestly. "I understand completely, and I want you to know that I did all that *during* office hours."

—•—

"My father works with five thousand people under him," bragged young Tommy.

"Oh, yeah? Just what does your father do?"

"He cuts grass in the cemetery."

—•—

A young immigrant managed to get a job as a janitor in a burlesque house. The boss told him it was his job to see to it that things were kept clean. The young man did a good job and payed particular attention to the dressing rooms. The girls were delighted and told the manager that the place had never looked so good. However, payday came and went, and the young man never came to collect.

Worried that he might lose such a hard worker, the manager sought the janitor out and asked him why he hadn't come for his pay.

The young man had trouble understanding at first, and then he asked in incredulous and broken English, "You mean I get wages, too?"

—•—

A foreman was watching a new man on the job. Every other man would pick up two sacks and carry them with him, but the new man picked up only one at a time. Thinking perhaps the new man couldn't manage the weight of both sacks, the foreman stopped him and inquired why he was carrying only one sack at a time.

"Don't worry, boss. I guess those other guys are just too lazy to make two trips like me."

—•—

"Tell me, Mr. Wright," said the personnel director, "why did you leave your last job?"

"Because of sickness, sir," replied Mr. Wright. "My boss got sick of me."

JUSTICE

The prisoner faced the court.

"What's the charge?" asked the judge.

"Drunk and disorderly."

"How do you plead?"

"Not guilty, your honor. I'm as sober as a judge."

"Guilty," said the judge. "Next case."

—•—

The witness on the stand was a gorgeous blonde with a dubious reputation. The prosecuting attorney was determined to discredit her as a witness.

"Tell me, madam," he said sternly, "where were you the night before last?"

"I was out with a gentleman friend," she replied.

"And where were you last night?"

"I was out with a gentleman friend."

By this time the judge, who was carried away by her beauty, asked softly, "Where will you be tonight?"

The prosecuting attorney was on his feet immediately. "Objection!" he shouted. "That was *my* next question."

KANGAROOS

"Oh, what ever shall I do?" wailed Emily the kangaroo.

"What's wrong?" asked her friend Mabel.

"I can't find my baby," replied Emily. "I've looked everywhere, but he's gone."

"Why, that's terrible," said Mabel. "You'd better call the police and tell them what happened."

"That's a good idea," agreed Emily. "Just one thing, though. Should I report a kidnapper or a *pickpocket?*"

KIDS

You can imagine the minister's dismay when two of his children got into a brawl while the church elders were having tea at the parsonage one Sunday afternoon.

"Children," he said, "remember the Golden Rule."

"I remember it, Daddy," replied his little daughter. "But Billy did unto me first."

—•—

An irate father broke up a fight between his two sons and demanded to know who started it.

"I thought I had made it clear that I will tolerate no fighting," he shouted. "Now, which one of you started it?"

"He did," replied his number-one son. "It wasn't a fight until he hit me back."

—●—

Two little girls were sitting at a crowded lunch counter located in a busy department store during the Christmas rush.

One little girl spoke up in a loud, clear voice, "You know, you're right. It is harder to be an angel than a virgin."

Her observation stopped the surrounding lunchers cold until the second little girl replied, "I know, the angel has almost all the lines."

—●—

A teen-age boy was searching frantically through the stacks for a book he had taken out of the library a few weeks before. Several of the librarians were helping him look, since they could not help being impressed with his determination to find the book. Finally one of them found it and presented it to him with a flourish.

"If you will take it to the front desk," she said, "I will check it out for you."

"Oh, no," he replied, "I don't want to take it out. It will just take a minute to find what I want."

"Well, then, perhaps you would like to take it into the reading room."

"No, that won't be necessary. You see, all I want to do is copy this number off the front page."

"It must be an important statistic for you to go to so much trouble."

"You might call it that, ma'am," he replied. "It's my girl's new unlisted phone number."

—●—

Mrs. Klein heard a fearful ruckus outside her door. Naturally she went out to see what was going on. Her daughter Sophie, age six, was running through the yard screaming her head off while the little boy who lived down the block was chasing her with a very mean look in his eye. Mrs. Klein caught the two of them and demanded to know why Jimmy was chasing her daughter.

"Because she hit me, that's why. And when I catch her, I'm going to clobber her."

"Sophie, did you hit Jimmy?" demanded her mother.

"Yes," replied Sophie calmly.

"But why?"

"So he'd chase me."

—●—

"What does your daddy do?" inquired the teacher of young Billy.

"My daddy follows the medical profession," replied the youngster.

"You mean he's a doctor?"

"No, ma'am, an undertaker."

—●—

Little Jimmy had never met his paternal grandmother, and since he was now five years old, she decided to make the trip from Des Moines to Los Angeles to make the acquaintance of her only grandchild. Due to a mix-up, she took a cab to her son's house only to be told by the baby-sitter that they had gone off to the airport to pick her up. She decided that it might be best to wait for them to come home before meeting her grandson, so she sat down in the living room to wait. However, Jimmy woke up from his nap and made his way into the living room.

"Who are you?" he demanded.

"I am your grandmother on your father's side," she replied.

"Oh, that's too bad," said little Jim.

"What ever do you mean, child?" his grandma asked.

"Well, from the way things are around here I can tell you right now, you're on the wrong side."

—●—

"Carrie, why did Mary and Joseph take Jesus with them to Jerusalem?"

The little girl shifted in her seat and said shyly, "I guess they couldn't get a baby-sitter."

—●—

Jimmy and his brother John were helping their father move some furniture. The two boys were instructed to move a wardrobe from one part of the house to another. Soon there were grunts and groans galore coming from the boys. Thinking that the job might prove too much for them, their father went down to lend a helping hand. There was Jimmy pushing and pulling at the huge closet, but John was nowhere in sight.

"Jimmy, where is your brother? Why isn't he helping you?"

"Oh, he is, Dad."

"Nonsense! I don't see him."

"Of course you don't see him, Dad. He's inside carrying the coat hangers."

—•—

Conversation between two kindergarteners:

"When I grow up, I'm going to marry a doctor. That way I can be sick for nothing."

"That's nothing. When I grow up, I'm going to marry a minister. Then I can be good for nothing."

—•—

A little boy was waiting for a train with his mother at Grand Central Station. To amuse the boy his mother gave him a penny and took him to a scale which told fortunes. Before the child could step on the scale, an enormous, fat woman pushed past him, stepped on the scale, and deposited her coin. Apparently the scale was not working, for her weight was registered at twenty pounds.

The little boy read the figures and said in an awed voice, "Look, Mommy, that lady is hollow."

—•—

I suppose everything changes, but I miss some of the old-fashioned, homey touches. When I was a kid, my mother used to come in every night and tuck me in. But my kids are all very modern. Every one of them has an electric blanket. My wife goes around every night to *plug* them in.

—•—

"Sally, I think you forgot the dot over the *i*," said the teacher to a little girl just learning to write.

"I didn't forget," little Sally assured her. "It's still in the pencil."

—•—

Little Alice was the minister's daughter, and everyone agreed that she was a very pretty child. But everyone also agreed that little

Penelope, the doctor's daughter, was the prettiest child in the whole county—possibly in the whole state. Naturally, this did not sit very well with little Alice. After hearing her very own aunt exclaiming over the beauty of the doctor's daughter, little Alice was moved to say, "But, Aunt Meg, it just isn't fair! He kept the best one for himself."

—•—

"Has your baby brother learned to talk yet?"

"Oh, sure," replied little Mike. "Now Mommy and Daddy are teaching him to keep quiet."

—•—

"Mommy," said little Charlie. "If you give a horse some water to drink, do you say, 'I am going to water the horse'?"

"That's right, dear," replied his mother.

"Well, I guess I'll go milk the cat."

—•—

"Can anyone tell me what it is that comes in like a lion but goes out like a lamb?" asked Miss Pringle.

"I know," said little Wendy, her star pupil. "It's my father."

—•—

The subject for discussion in class was proverbs.

"Can anyone give me a proverb about parents?" asked the teacher. "How about a proverb about fathers?"

Little Clarissa raised her hand. "My mommy has a proverb about my daddy," she informed the class. "There's no fool like an old fool."

—•—

One veteran father of nine claims he has a surefire method for putting babies to sleep. He just tosses them up in the air and catches them a few times. Claims it works like a charm. Of course, he admits to having very low ceilings.

—•—

A well-dressed man and his small daughter went shopping in a fashionable department store. Of course, it wasn't long before the little girl was informing her father in a determined voice that she "had to go." Her father didn't know quite what to do, and his daughter was most insistent. However, a saleslady came to his rescue.

"It's all right, sir," she said. "I'll be happy to take her."

Greatly relieved, he handed over his little girl, and about five minutes later she and the saleslady returned.

"Now, Gloria," said the grateful parent, "don't forget to thank this nice lady."

Little Gloria had other ideas. "Why should I have to thank her, Daddy?" asked the child. "She had to go, too."

"I always know when summer is here," moaned one weary mother of four preschoolers.

"How's that?" inquired her neighbor.

"Summer is here when the kids start slamming all the doors they forget to close all winter long."

"Grandpa," said young Bill, "why do people say 'There's no fool like an old fool'?"

"I guess," replied the old man, "it's because folks know you just can't beat experience."

After reading the story of Jonah and the whale to her Sunday school class, Miss Parker decided to give them a little quiz.

"What," she asked "is the moral of this story?" For the answer she called on little Timmy Brown.

Timmy thought for a minute and then replied, "People make whales throw up."

Johnny, the minister's son, was watching his father labor over Sunday's sermon.

"Daddy, I thought you said that God tells you what to say every Sunday."

"He does, son," replied his father.

"Then how come you cross so much of it out?"

Two kids were amusing themselves one rainy afternoon by beating on some empty pots and pans and pretending that they were a marching band. After about an hour one little boy said to the other, "I wish Mommy would come and make us stop. This noise is killing me."

—•—

A Sunday school teacher was explaining the concept of Judgment Day to her class. She went on at great length trying to impress on her class the idea that we would all be rewarded or punished according to all our deeds here on earth. And of course those of us who make it will wear crowns of glory.

"Now," she asked, "who will wear the biggest crowns of glory?"

The class thought about it for a minute, and little Sally came up with the logical answer. "The ones with the biggest heads."

—•—

"You know, I don't think my mother ever loved me."

"What makes you say that?"

"Well, for one thing, she used to wrap my lunch in a road map."

—•—

A young mother was shocked at the language she overheard her little boy using one afternoon. Determined to be fair, she decided to give the child a chance to explain, so she inquired, "Billy, where did you ever hear such words?"

"From Barbara," he replied. "She says them all the time."

Just to be on the safe side Billy's mother decided to have a little chat with Barbara. The next afternoon at the playground she confronted the child and inquired, "Barbara, do you use bad words?"

"Who told you?" asked Barbara.

"Oh, a little bird told me."

"Well, how do you like that?" demanded the child. "And after all the bread crumbs I've given the little bastards."

—•—

Mama came home early one evening from her bridge game to find her teen-age daughter in what used to be called a "compromising position" with her boyfriend on the living-room couch.

"Well, I never . . ." exclaimed the startled parent.

"But, Mother," protested her daughter, "you *must* have!"

—•—

A magazine salesman made a stop at the Klinger residence. A little boy answered his knock on the door.

"Let me speak to your mother, sonny," said the salesman.

"She ain't home," said the boy.

"Then let me speak to your father."

"He ain't home either."

"Is there anybody else at home I can speak to?" asked the impatient salesman.

"My sister."

"Would you mind bringing her to the door?"

The little boy vanished into the house and left the salesman cooling his heels on the doorstep for about ten minutes. Finally he came back alone.

"Where's your sister?" demanded the salesman. "I thought you were going to bring her to the door."

"I tried," said the little boy. "But I couldn't lift her out of her playpen."

—●—

Overheard at a Beverly Hills birthday party:

"My father can lick your father."

"Don't be silly. My father *is* your father!"

—●—

Sally was crazy about school, but her little brother was considerably less enthusiastic.

"Let's play school," said Sally one rainy Saturday afternoon.

"Okay," agreed her brother, "but let's play I'm absent."

—●—

"Mommy, our new teacher asked me if I had any brothers or sisters."

"What did you say?"

"I said I was an only child."

"And what did she say?"

"Thank God!"

—●—

"I hope I didn't see you copying from Jimmy's test paper," said the teacher.

"I hope you didn't either," replied her pupil.

—●—

"Johnny, how old would your parents be if they had been born in 1930?"

"That depends," replied the child.

"What do you mean 'that depends'?" asked the confused teacher.

"On whether you want to know how old my father would be or if you want to know how old my mother would be."

—●—

"Teacher," said little Bertie, "I can't do this problem because I ain't got no pencil."

"Now, Bertie," she said, "it's 'I don't have a pencil.' 'You don't have a pencil.' 'We don't have any pencils.' 'They don't have any pencils.' Do you understand?"

"No," admitted Bertie. "What happened to all them pencils?"

—●—

A Sunday school teacher was trying to impress his class with the concept of kindness to all of God's creatures.

"For example," he said, "if I were to stop a man from beating his mule, what virtue would I be exhibiting?"

"Brotherly love," replied young Bill in a hopeful tone.

—●—

Two little boys were trying to cross a busy intersection. They waited patiently for a green light, but it hardly mattered. Cars ran red lights and whizzed through the intersection with no regard for either the speed limit or the crowd of pedestrians. Several times the two boys tried to cross only to be forced back by the traffic.

"Tell me," said one little boy to his friend, "what do you want to be *if* you grow up?"

—●—

An enthusiastic young teacher made a point of reading the works of the great poets to her third-grade class. She would select a new poet each week and expect her class to learn something about each poet's life as well as his work. This particular week she had settled on Milton, the blind English poet.

On Friday she inquired of her class, "Tell me, what was Milton's great affliction?" For the answer she called on young Mike.

"He was a poet," replied Mike simply.

—●—

A little girl was telling her grandmother about her first time in church.

"Were you a good girl, Sally?"

"Oh, yes, Gran."

"Did you mind your manners?"

"I sure did, Gran. This man offered me a whole plate full of money, and I took only one little piece."

—•—

A little boy was telling his friend about his big sister's new baby.

"There's only one thing that bothers me," said the puzzled child. "They haven't told me if it's a boy or a girl, so I don't know if I'm an uncle or an aunt."

—•—

Young Richard's father was a member of three lodges.

"You know," bragged Richard to his friend Bobby, "my daddy is a Lion, a Moose, and an Elk."

"Gee," said Bobby, his eyes wide, "if I give you a quarter, can I see him?"

—•—

Every Sunday morning little Peggy's mother would give her two dimes. One ten-cent piece was for the collection plate at Sunday school. The other was Peggy's to spend as she liked. One Sunday morning while Peggy was skipping along on her way to church, the two coins clutched in her hand suddenly flew into the air and then hit the ground. One dime lay safely on the pavement, but the other rolled down the street and finally dropped into a grating. Horror-stricken, Peggy inspected the grating from every angle and finally realized that the coin was lost forever. She stood lost in thought for a moment and then raised her eyes heavenward and said, "Dear Lord, I'm sorry, but there went your dime."

—•—

It was late Friday night when Mrs. Burns finally managed to get her son bedded down for the night. She stumbled wearily into the toy-strewn living room and sank into the nearest chair. After a few minutes of silent reflection her face brightened.

"John," she said to her equally exhausted spouse, "tomorrow is Saturday. Why don't you take Johnny to the zoo?"

"What do you mean, *take* him?" came the reply. "If they want him, they can come and get him."

—•—

Young Sally came home from Sunday school with a puzzled expression. "Mommy, my Sunday school teacher says we are here to help 'others.' Is that true?"

"Yes, darling."

"But then what are the 'others' here for?"

—•—

Two boys were watching an old rooster chase a spring chicken around the coop. Suddenly the farmer's wife appeared and threw a few handfuls of corn on the ground. The rooster stopped his chase and started pecking at the corn.

"I do declare," said one of the boys, "I hope I never live to see the day that I'll be *that* hungry."

—•—

Six-year-old Mary came home in a flood of tears. "Kenny broke my doll," she sobbed.

"How did it happen?" demanded her outraged mother.

"He wouldn't give me a piece of his cake, so I hit him over the head with it."

—•—

Little Freddy went to visit his Aunt Jane. It was his very first time away from home, and after trying his best to be brave about it, the boy burst into tears.

"What's the matter, darling?" said his aunt. "Are you homesick?"

"No," sobbed little Fred. "I think I'm *heresick*."

KINDNESS

There is an aging Hollywood producer who has long since given up the corny old "casting couch" approach. But he still has all the girls he can handle. He simply let it get around town that his health wasn't very good and the doctors had informed him that too much excitement just might kill him. He also let it be known that since he had no family, he had made out a will leaving everything he owned (which was considerable) to whoever might be with him at the moment of his death. And now it seems that there is just no end to the number of girls who are trying to *kill him with kindness*.

KNOWLEDGE

Two young men who had grown up in the same town were lifelong rivals. They competed for the same school honors, the same girl, and the same job, and they finally found themselves in competition for the honor of becoming senior Sunday school teacher.

Meeting one morning on the train, one said to the other, "Why do you want to be a Sunday school teacher at all? I'll wager you don't even know the Lord's Prayer!"

"Don't be absurd," snapped his rival. "It's 'Now I lay me down to sleep. . . .' "

"Okay, you win," admitted the first, "but I never knew you knew so much about the Bible."

LANGUAGE

Two sheep were grazing in a pasture.
The first sheep said "Baaa."
His companion replied "Moo."
The first sheep was rather startled. "What are you doing?" he asked. "Sheep don't say 'Moo'; they say Baaa.' "
"I know," replied his friend. "I was just practicing a foreign language."

LAUNDRIES

"You know," said Mr. Jones, "I think I'd better change laundries. The one I'm using has taken to sending back my shirts with different buttons sewed on."

"You think that's bad," replied Mr. Smith. "My laundry has been sending me back my buttons with different shirts sewn on."

LAWYERS

An old Indian was arrested and taken into court on charges of running a still. The judge asked the Indian for his name, but the

Indian gave no sign of having heard the question. The judge then asked if the Indian had a lawyer, but this question drew no response. The judge was a busy man, and since there was no real evidence that the Indian sold what he made, the judge told the D.A. that he was going to dismiss the case. The judge told the Indian he could go and called the next case. The Indian sat motionless while the next defendant was brought in and charged with operating a still. The defendant's lawyer went into a two-hour defense, and when he was through, the judge sentenced his client to three years' hard labor. The lawyer gathered up his notes and started to leave the courtroom when the old Indian got up, walked over to him, and whispered, "White man talk too much."

—●—

Two lawyers got into a name-calling session before the trial began.

"You are a dirty, lying, crooked ambulance-chaser," snarled the first lawyer.

"And you," snapped the second, "are a two-bit political appointee and a shyster to boot."

"Well," said the judge, "now that you've both been identified, I guess I can proclaim this court in session."

—●—

The prisoner faced the bench. "Tell me," said the judge, "have you anything to offer this court before it passes sentence?"

"No, your honor," replied the prisoner, "my lawyer took my last cent."

—●—

The Devil and St. Peter were having an argument over the wall that separates heaven from hell. It was crumbling in several places, and St. Peter insisted that it was the Devil's job to repair it.

"If you don't repair this wall in one week's time, I am going to sue you," snarled St. Peter.

"Oh, really? And where, may I ask," snorted the Devil, "do you think you're going to find a lawyer?"

—●—

A woman on the witness stand kept prefacing her remarks with the phrase "I think." The prosecuting attorney was outraged and demanded that the woman stop telling the court what she thought and start telling them what she knew. The woman was very apologetic, but as she admitted to the judge, "I'm sorry, your honor. I'm not a lawyer. I can't talk without thinking."

—●—

Mr. Schwartz, of the legal firm of O'Hara and Schwartz, was hired to defend a man accused of murdering his wife. Schwartz spent many weeks preparing a defense, but at the last minute he was called out of town. Before leaving he turned the case over to his partner, O'Hara, and carefully explained his proposed defense. Mr. Schwartz then left town, and Mr. O'Hara went to court. A few weeks later O'Hara cabled Schwartz, concerning the case, "Justice has triumphed."

Mr. Schwartz wired back, "Tough break. Appeal at once."

LAZINESS

A guy walked into a bar and said, "I'll give one thousand dollars to the laziest man in this saloon."

A fellow who was lounging on a nearby bench replied, "Okay, mister. I'm your man."

"But how can I be sure?" asked his would-be benefactor. "Are you sure you are the laziest man in this saloon?"

"I sure am," he replied. "Now would you mind rolling me over and sticking the money in my back pocket?"

LEGS

Two show girls were chatting. "My mother always told me that money doesn't grow on trees," said the first.

"That is very true," replied her friend as she crossed her lovely legs. "But there are some *limbs* that have a way of attracting it."

LIARS

There was a very poor sheepherder out in Montana. Year after year he and his family struggled through the winter, never quite going broke but never making much profit either. One spring morning the sheepherder's wife decided that her husband and three sons needed some new underwear. But need them or not, there just wasn't any money for new ones. So she bought a package of red dye and mixed up a batch in a tub in the backyard. While she was inside gathering up her menfolk's longjohns, a little lamb came gamboling through the yard and landed with a splash right in the vat of dye. The woman dashed out and rescued the now bright-red lamb. A few days later a buyer happened to spot the lamb and thinking it some new breed, paid the sheepherder ten times what the lamb was worth. About a week later another buyer who had heard rumors of a new breed put in his order for a couple of red lambs. The sheepherder's wife obligingly dyed a pair, and they sold them at quite a profit. Well, soon orders for red lambs were pouring in from all over the country, and the sheepherder and his family can afford all the new underwear they want. As a matter of fact, they're the biggest lamb dyers in the whole state of Montana.

LIBRARIANS

A little old lady appeared at the librarian's desk and asked if she could recommend a book. The librarian thought for a moment and then suggested a book about a cardinal.

"Oh no," said the little lady, "I'm not interested in books on religion."

"But you don't understand," said the librarian. "This cardinal is a real bird."

"Well," replied the little old lady, "I wouldn't be interested in his *private* life either."

LIES

"Boy, is my wife going to be sorry," said one man bitterly to his companion. "She really has nerve to think I'd believe a story like that."

"What happened?" asked his friend.

"Last night my wife didn't come home at all, and this morning when I asked her where she had been, she told me she spent the night with her sister Blanche."

"Well, how do you know she didn't?" asked his friend.

"I'll tell you how I know," he replied angrily. "I know because I spent the night with her sister Blanche."

—●—

"You know, they have a machine today that can tell if a man is telling the truth or not."

"Did you ever see one, Jake?"

"See one! Hell, I married one!"

LINEUP

"Oh, officer," cooed the sweet young thing to the policeman who accompanied her while she looked over the men in the lineup, "I think that he's the man who molested me, but maybe you'd better make him do it over again so I can be sure."

LOGIC

Mrs. Kline and Mrs. O'Shea were discussing their children.

"My boy Irving is coming home from prison next week," said Mrs. Kline.

"Why, that's wonderful!" said Mrs. O'Shea. "But I thought he had another year to serve."

"They gave him a year off for good behavior."

"Well," said Mrs. O'Shea, "you can certainly be proud to know you've got such a *good* son."

—●—

Three co-eds were taking a course in logic. During one of the lectures the professor posed a problem in reasoning. "Let us suppose," said the professor, "that you are all alone, adrift on a raft on the high seas. Suddenly you are confronted with an ocean liner with hundreds of sex-starved crewmen on board. How would you react in this situation in order to avoid any problems that might arise?"

The redhead spoke first. "I would try to turn my raft in the opposite direction."

The brunette was next. "I would pretend that I was one of those intrepid adventurers who cross the sea alone on a raft."

But the blonde had other thoughts. "Well, professor," she said, "I surely do understand the *situation,* but I fail to see the *problem.*"

—●—

A census taker approached a farmhouse up in the hills of Tennessee where he was greeted by a six-year-old girl.

"Tell me, child, how many are in your family?" the census taker asked.

"Four," replied the little girl. "My mama, my daddy, my sister, and me."

"Well, where is your daddy?"

"Oh," replied the girl, "I reckon he's gone fishin' 'cause he put on his rubber boots, and it ain't rainin'."

"Well, may I speak to your mother?"

"Nope. She must be over on the next farm. The catalog's gone, and mama cain't read."

"Well, then, I'll just have to talk to your sister."

"Sure thing," replied the little girl. "I reckon she's down at the barn with our hired man. There ain't but two things she likes to do, and we already ate supper."

—•—

Harvey fell madly in love with a Las Vegas show girl. He finally broke down and told her how he felt. He pleaded with her to be his girl.

"Okay," she agreed, "but I want furs, jewelry, a new apartment, a maid, and flowers every day."

"Anything at all," said the smitten Harvey.

The more he spent on her, the more he loved her. One day he arrived at her apartment with a diamond ring as big as a poker chip.

"Darling," he said, "I love you, I adore you, I want to marry you."

"Are you nuts?" she replied. "Do you think I'd marry anyone who throws his money around the way you do?"

—•—

"Mommy, are you the closest relative I've got?" asked five-year-old Susan.

"Yes, dear," replied her mother. "Your father is in the basement."

—•—

"How can you tell if these are mushrooms or toadstools?"

"Well, you could try eating a few before you go to bed. If you wake up tomorrow, they're mushrooms."

—•—

Mr. Katz was having his new suit fitted by his lifelong friend Mr. Cohen. While he was waiting, a well-dressed man came in, selected two suits from a rack, and left with them.

"You know," said Mr. Katz, "I've seen that man coming in here for years, but I've never seen him pay you a nickel."

"Well," reasoned Mr. Cohen, "his credit must be good. Look at the beautiful clothes he wears."

—•—

A psychiatrist was examining a patient to determine his sanity. "Tell me what you would think if you lost one of your ears," said the doctor.

"I would think it would be a terrible misfortune," replied the patient.

"And what would you think if you lost both your ears?"

"I think it would be a disaster. Why, I'd be almost blind."

"Now, why would you be blind if you lost both your ears?" inquired the doctor anxiously.

"Because I wouldn't be able to wear my glasses," replied the patient with patient logic.

—•—

A woman who had committed her husband to a mental institution was talking to the chief of staff. "How will we know when my Harry is well again, Doctor?"

"We have a simple test we give all our patients," he replied. "We put a hose into a trough, turn on the water, give the patient a bucket, and then tell him to empty out the trough."

"What does that prove?" inquired the woman.

"Elementary, madam," the doctor assured her. "Any sane person will turn off the hose."

"Isn't science wonderful?" she replied. "I never would have thought of that."

—•—

"Six dollars!" exclaimed the woman as she checked out of the supermarket with two very small packages. "Why, that's highway robbery. The owner must be crazy to charge prices like that."

"No, ma'am," replied the cashier, "the boss ain't crazy. He's a philosopher."

"What do you mean 'philosopher'?" demanded the lady.

"Well," replied the cashier, "he figures that if you can't take it with you, you might as well leave it *here*."

—•—

A wife was busy convincing her husband that she really did need the new dress she had just purchased. "Look at it this way, darling," she reasoned. "The dress was originally a hundred dollars. I bought it when it was marked down to fifty. So I really bought the dress with the fifty dollars I saved."

LOVE

"John," sighed his new bride, "how did you first realize that you loved me?"

"It was easy," replied her tactless spouse. "I started getting mad when people told me you were dumb and ugly."

—●—

Myrtle was telling Sadie about her new boyfriend. "Sadie, it was love at second sight."

"Wait a minute, Myrtle. Don't you mean love at first sight?"

"No, how could it be? I didn't know he was rich when we first met."

—●—

The dean of women at a small New England college was lecturing her students on moral virtues.

"In moments of great temptation," she said, "just ask yourself one question: Is this hour of sinful pleasure worth a lifetime of disgrace?" Having said her piece, the dean then asked if there were any questions.

One pretty young girl raised her hand and asked quietly, "Can you really make it last an *hour*?"

—●—

"I just had a talk with our superintendent," said the husband as he came back to his apartment, "and that nut actually told me that he had made love to every woman in this building except one. Can you believe that?"

"Hmmmmmm," mused his wife thoughtfully, "I'll bet it's that snooty Mrs. Hunter on the tenth floor."

—●—

A gorgeous young girl got into the elevator and asked to be taken to the penthouse home of the very rich, very eccentric Mr. Van Horn. About three hours later the elevator operator got a call from the penthouse and arrived just in time to hear this tender parting: "Good night, Mr. Van Horn. I've had a wonderful time—unless the check bounces."

—●—

A distraught woman went to a marriage counselor. "You've just got to help me," she cried. "I love him. He loves me. We like the same books, the same music, the same films. When we're apart, we're miserable. I don't know what to do."

"But I don't think I understand," replied the counselor. "From what you tell me you two are perfectly compatible and very much in love. Just what is the problem?"

"What's the problem?" asked the woman incredulously. "The problem is what should I tell my husband."

—●—

"Darling," he murmured into the phone, "I love you. I adore you. I'd climb Mount Everest in my bare feet for you. I'd slay dragons for you. I'd walk on hot coals for you. I would endure any hardship for you."

"Oh, Ralphie. I love you, too. When will I see you again?"

"Well," replied her valiant lover, "I'll pick you up on Saturday if it doesn't rain."

—●—

A love-struck young man gazed upon his beloved and sighed, "Darling, I have loved you more than you will ever know." With that his companion drew herself up and slapped him right across the face.

"You rat!" she cried. "You did take advantage of me when I got drunk last night."

—●—

"Daddy," said young David, "what's puppy love?"
"The beginning of a dog's life, my boy."

—●—

"That's some nurse," said the patient to a young intern who was making his rounds. "Why, just the touch of her hand cooled my fever."

"Yes, I know," said the intern. "I heard the slap all the way at the other end of the hall."

—●—

Miss Henshaw, a spinster lady, was invited to chaperon a sleigh ride. The other chaperon was to be the eligible minister of a nearby church. As they were racing through the winter night, surrounded by amorous young couples, Miss Henshaw heaved a great sigh.

"Why, whatever is the matter?" asked the minister.

"Oh, it's just that nobody loves me, and besides my hands are cold."

"Nonsense," replied the minister earnestly. "God loves you, and you can sit on your hands."

—●—

"I'm not rich, I don't own a yacht and a lot of fancy cars like Myron Stevens, but I love you, Beverly," said the young man.

"I love you, too, dear," replied Beverly, "but tell me more about Myron Stevens."

LUCK

"Boy, is my big sister lucky!" said little Marvin to his friend.

"How come?"

"Well, last night she went to a party where they played kissing games. The boy had to either kiss a girl or give her a box of candy. And *my* sister came home with a dozen boxes."

MAIDEN LADIES

A couple of unmarried schoolteachers decided that when they retired, they would pool their resources and buy a chicken farm. When the time came, they bought their farm and went to visit the local poultry dealer.

"We want to buy three hundred hens and three hundred roosters," they informed the dealer.

The dealer was amused, but being an honest man, he said, "Three hundred hens will start you off real well, but really, ladies, you don't need three hundred roosters."

"We understand that," the ladies assured him, "but we also know what it is to be lonesome."

MARRIAGE

Two young men were discussing a mutual friend's marriage. "You know," said one, "I had dinner with old George and his new bride last week."

"Really, how was it?"

"Not so bad. I'm sending them a new carving set. As a matter of fact, I'm going to stop off at the hardware store and pick it up tonight."

"You bought a carving set in a hardware store?" asked his disbelieving friend.

"Of course," he replied. "Where else would I buy a mallet and a chisel?"

—●—

A long-married couple were having dinner with a pair of newlyweds. "You know," said the older wife, "a man is not *complete* until he is married. Isn't that right, Henry?"

Her husband, Henry, smiled and replied, "Quite right, my dear. Once a man is married, he's *really* finished."

—●—

That girl has been married so many times she'd save time at her weddings if she'd just keep the bouquet and throw the groom away.

—●—

Two vacationing merchants from the garment center were reclining on a beach in Miami. Their conversation turned to a beautiful movie star who was staying at their hotel.

"Look," said the first. "If you take away that gorgeous figure, that beautiful blonde hair, those expensive clothes, and that perfect face, then what's left?"

"My wife" came the grim reply.

—●—

A recently divorced man was feeling so depressed he decided to consult a psychiatrist. The doctor listened to his complaints and then had this to recommend. "I think you ought to get married again, Mr. Jones. Buy a house, have some kids, live like other men. You'll be back to your old self in no time."

"No thanks, Doc," said Mr. Jones. "I'd rather commit suicide."

—●—

A harried husband was driving his wife and her friend to their bridge game.

"Tell me, Harriet, why does your husband always stick his hand out the window while he's driving?"

"Because," replied Harriet, "that way everybody knows the worm is ready to turn."

—●—

A henpecked husband finally managed to lie his way out of the house one Thursday night. He joined a few of his friends for a poker game that went on far into the night. When the game finally broke up, he was horrified to learn that it was four o'clock in the morning. He was sure his wife would murder him, but a sudden flash of genius saved his neck. He called his home and roused his sleepy wife. "Don't pay the ransom," he shouted jubilantly. "I've escaped."

—●—

Why is planning a vacation always easy for a married man?

Because his boss will tell him when and his wife will tell him where.

—●—

Henry and Myrtle had been married for six months when they moved into their new house. "I just want you to know," said Myrtle, "that if it weren't for my money, we wouldn't be here."

A few months later as the last of the new furniture was being delivered, she said, "You know, if it weren't for my money, this furniture wouldn't be here."

The day the new color TV was delivered she kept right on rubbing it in. "If it weren't for my money, this TV wouldn't be here."

"Myrtle," said Harry wearily, "I think you ought to know something. If it weren't for your money, *I* wouldn't be here."

—●—

Fred and Jake were discussing their jealous wives. "My wife is so jealous," said Fred, "she goes over all my shirts looking for traces of lipstick."

"You think that's bad," said Jake. "My wife goes over all my clothes looking for long blonde hairs."

"Does she ever find any?" asked Fred.

"No, but that doesn't mean she trusts me," said Jake. "Last night she accused me of going out with bald-headed women."

—•—

"Just tell me one thing, Ethel," demanded her outraged husband. "Where does all that money I give you for food get to?"

"Just stand sideways and look in the mirror!" snapped his wife.

—•—

Mrs. Lee and Mrs. Klein met in the hospital one day. "Tell me," said Mrs. Lee, "how is your husband? I hear he was in an accident. Is he all right?"

"Well," replied Mrs. Klein, "he ain't all right, but he's just like he was before."

—•—

A traveling salesman (who must have been a home-loving type at heart) finished up his business on the road a day earlier than expected, so he sent his wife a wire saying that he'd be home that evening instead of the following day. He then proceeded to drive three hundred miles to his hometown. However, when he arrived, he was horrified to find his wife in bed with another man. He was stunned and only just managed to get out of the house without committing murder. The next day his mother-in-law tracked him down to the hotel where he was staying and pleaded with him to at least listen to her daughter's side of the story. The salesman insisted that he was too upset to have any conversation with his wife. But his mother-in-law prevailed, and he finally agreed that he would listen to his wife's side of it—but only if his mother-in-law was the one to do the talking. She agreed and told him that she would call him as soon as she got the story. About an hour later his mother-in-law called him back. "I knew she had a perfectly good explanation," she said triumphantly. "She never got your telegram."

—•—

"Just what the hell are you two doing?" bellowed the enraged husband when he came upon his wife in bed with another man.

"You see," said his wife to her paramour, "I told you he was stupid."

—•—

The district attorney turned to face the woman sitting on the witness stand. "Now, Mrs. Rutledge, would you tell this court why you shot your husband with a bow and arrow?"

"Because," replied Mrs. Rutledge, "I didn't want to wake the children."

—•—

A disenchanted husband was watching his wife get undressed. She removed her wig, her false eyelashes, her makeup, her padded bra, and her girdle, and what was left prompted her spouse to say, "You know, Ethel, you're not the girl I married. In fact, you never were."

—•—

Two women were talking. One complained bitterly about her husband's snoring. She said it was driving her crazy and that she was at her wit's end. Her friend was completely sympathetic.

"I know how you must feel, my dear. Only think of my poor sister."

"What's your sister got to do with it?" asked her friend.

"Well, you see, my sister's husband was a very heavy snorer. And it finally did drive her mad. You see, she was married to a ventriloquist, and he snored on her side of the bed."

—•—

A popular Southern belle whose beauty had made her one of the most sought-after women in the state of Louisiana finally accepted the proposal of one of her most persistent suitors.

"How does it feel to be engaged?" asked one of her closest friends.

"I feel just like a man must feel after he has built up his business and then finds himself about to go into the hands of a receiver," she replied.

—•—

"I didn't like the looks of that girl you hired as the upstairs maid, Jack," said his wife. "I fired her this afternoon."

"You mean you fired her without even giving her a chance?" asked Jack.

"No, dear," was her determined reply, "without giving *you* a chance."

—●—

Two young girls were talking about their boyfriends. "Are you really going to marry Albert?" asked one.

"I can't make up my mind," replied her friend. "I know he's fast and loose now, but he says if I'll marry him, he'll be just the opposite."

"Well, then, what are you waiting for?" asked her friend. "Don't you believe him?"

"Oh, I believe him all right," replied the girl. "But I'm not sure that I want to be married to a man who is slow and tight."

—●—

A man of ninety-five informed his doctor that he was planning on marrying a twenty-two-year-old nightclub entertainer.

"I hope you realize that this could be fatal," said his doctor.

"I wish you hadn't said that, Doc," said the old man. "I'd feel real bad now if she dies."

—●—

"And another thing," she fumed. "Married men live longer than single men. You should be grateful that you married me."

"My dear" came the bitter reply, "married men don't really live longer. It only *seems* that way."

—●—

Customer: "I want to buy a pair of cheap shoes."
Sarcastic clerk: "To go with what?"
Customer: "My cheap husband."

—●—

"I know just the type of man I want to marry, but he won't be easy to find," said Irene.

"What kind of a man is that?"

"One who's smart enough to make a lot of money and dumb enough to give most of it to me."

—●—

"Son, I just know you'll do the right thing by this little girl," said the preacher. "You just marry her, and you'll be at the end of your troubles." So he did the right thing, and he married the girl, and about six months later when he saw the preacher again he tried to murder him.

"You miserable liar!" shouted the young man. "You told me if I married her, I would be at the end of my troubles. Well, I married her, and she has made my life miserable."

"That may be true, son, but you can't blame me," replied the minister. "I said you'd be at the end of your troubles, but I never said which end."

—●—

Before Herman got married he always said he would be the boss or know the reason why. And now that Herman is married, what does he say? He knows the reason why.

—●—

After viewing some of the new "adult" movies Martha asked her husband, George, why he never made love to her the way the men in those movies made love.

"Are you serious?" replied her spouse. "Do you know how much they *pay* those guys to do that?"

—●—

"Miss Johnson, please draw a red circle around the twenty-seventh of the month on the calendar."

"Certainly, but what day is that?"

"That is the day my marriage occurred."

"Excuse me, sir," said Miss Johnson. "I don't mean to be rude, but a marriage 'takes place.' A disaster or a catastrophe 'occurs.' "

"As I said, Miss Johnson, that is the day my marriage occurred."

—●—

Two ladies were gossiping at the beauty parlor. "Did you hear about Mabel?"

"No, what about her?"

"Well, you remember how she was always after her husband to buy her a Jaguar?"

"Yes."

"Well, he did, and it ate her."

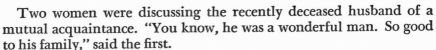

Two women were discussing the recently deceased husband of a mutual acquaintance. "You know, he was a wonderful man. So good to his family," said the first.

"Yes, he was," agreed her friend. "Why, he was hardly *ever* home."

—•—

A weary man dragged himself to his doctor's office. The doctor examined him and found the patient's condition alarming. He complained of sleepless nights, loss of appetite, fatigue, and constant tension.

"My good man," said the doctor, "I'm going to call your wife and tell her that you must go to the seashore for a complete rest."

"Well, Doc," said the patient with a weary sigh, "if you want me to get a *complete* rest you'd better tell *her* to go to the mountains."

—•—

Two old cronies were having a friendly drink one evening. "Tell me, Charlie, do you believe that marriage is like a lottery?"

"Hell, no!" said Charlie. "At least in a lottery a man has a chance."

—•—

"No," cooed the much-married international beauty, "it is definitely not true that I married my last husband because he was a millionaire. Actually I made him one."

"Really?" said the talk-show host. "What was he before?"

"A multimillionaire."

—•—

The sixth Mrs. Leo P. Quincy seemed inclined to be jealous of her five predecessors. But her husband comforted her with this thought.

"It is true that they were all my wives. But just think, my love. You will be my widow."

—●—

Sally had married the dreariest bore in town and went off to Niagara Falls (where else?) for her honeymoon. Two weeks later she was back in town looking positively radiant. "It was just wonderful," she gushed to a group of girl friends who had come over for coffee. "You just can't imagine how exciting it was."

Since every one of the girls present knew only too well the sort of bore she had married, it was difficult to imagine. So difficult that one was moved to say, "Why, what did you do? Go over the Falls in a barrel?"

—●—

Two men were discussing their marriages. "I never knew what real happiness was until I got married," said one.

"Yeah, I know what you mean," said the other. "But then it's too late."

—●—

You know, there really is such a thing as a happily married couple. It's any husband who's out with another man's wife.

—●—

"I really do love Henry," wailed June, "but I could never marry an atheist! Why, he doesn't believe in anything—not even in hell."

"Don't you worry, dear," soothed her mother. "You marry him, and we'll convince him."

—●—

"You don't understand," moaned George. "I can't eat, I can't sleep, I can't think straight. All I do is think of her. At night I even dream about her. I'm miserable," he groaned, "and she doesn't care."

"I know, I know," consoled his friend.

"How could you know? Have *you* ever been disappointed in love?" demanded George.

"Believe it or not, I have," confessed his friend. "Twice, as a matter of fact."

"You mean that you've been jilted twice?"

"Well, not exactly," said his friend. "I married the second one."

—●—

A young man and his bride-to-be went to a carnival one summer evening. They decided to have their palms read and ask the gypsy what the future held for them. The old gypsy looked deep into her crystal ball and slowly shook her head. They bent closer, eager to hear her words, but she would say nothing. This infuriated the younger woman, and she stormed out of the tent, leaving her fiancé alone with the fortune-teller.

"My son," she said, "I can do nothing for you, but if you would heed my words, go into the next tent and let Zoltan advise you."

"And who is Zoltan?" he asked.

"Zoltan is the greatest phrenologist in the world," she replied.

"And why do I need a phrenologist, old woman?"

"Because, my son, if you persist in this marriage, you need your head examined!"

—●—

Two friends were discussing the forthcoming marriage of a fraternity brother. "What a shame Sally and Bob aren't nearly good enough for each other," said the first with a grin.

"Whatever makes you say a thing like that?" asked his surprised friend.

"I have it on the best authority. I've been talking to *his* mother and *her* father."

—●—

Two secretaries were discussing the attributes of their ideal husbands. The first one insisted that her ideal mate be musically inclined, sing, dance, tell jokes, and above all, stay home with her every night.

Her friend thought it over for a minute and said, "Are you sure you want to get married? You'd be better off with a TV set."

—●—

"Why is a pretty girl like a melody?" asked little Mike.

"Well, son," replied his dad, "I guess it's because when you marry her, you've got to face the music."

—●—

"You can't be serious!" gasped Barbara. "You aren't really going to marry that crazy old man even if he is supposed to be a millionaire."

"Oh, yes, I am," replied Harriet firmly. "He may be cracked, but he's far from broke."

—•—

"Professor Peabody," inquired a young co-ed, "was the goddess Athena married?"

"My dear," replied the sage professor, "Athena was the goddess of wisdom. Naturally she remained single."

—•—

"Tell me, Aunt Emily, why is it you never married?" inquired a young man of his favorite aunt.

"Well, Charlie, I have a dog that snarls, a parrot that swears, a chimney that smokes, and a cat that stays out all night. I just never needed a husband."

—•—

Father: "I will not have you rushing Ruth into marriage! Give her time. She can wait until the right man comes along."

Mother: "Why should she? I didn't when I was her age!"

—•—

A man called the local mental hospital and demanded to know if any of the inmates had escaped that night.

"Not that I know of," replied the doctor who had answered the call. "Why do you ask?"

"Because," replied the caller, "some poor guy just ran away with my wife."

—•—

A man went to a rather unorthodox marriage counselor and complained bitterly that his wife seemed bored by their marriage. "I really love her, but she seems so indifferent to me," he said.

"Well, you might try this," said the counselor. "When you get home tonight, start making mad, passionate love to her as soon as you see her. It doesn't matter where it is—the living room, the kitchen, anyplace. It might surprise her out of her indifference to you."

The next morning the man called the counselor.

"What happened?"

"Well, I did what you told me. She opened the door, and I started making mad, passionate love to her just as soon as I got inside."

"Yes, but did it work? Did she seem any less indifferent to you?" asked the counselor.

"It was hard to tell in all that confusion. But I can tell you one thing. Her bridge club was sure surprised."

—●—

"I was a fool when I married you, Harvey!" snapped his shrewish wife.

"I know, I know," moaned Harvey, "but I was too infatuated to notice at the time."

—●—

"I know, sir, that it is a mere formality, but I would like your permission to marry your daughter Susan."

"And what makes you think getting my permission to marry Susan is a 'mere formality,' young man?" demanded the irate father.

"Susan's mother" was his calm reply.

—●—

"I bet you think twice before leaving that little wife of yours home alone at night," said Bill.

"You're absolutely right. First I think up a reason for going out, and then I think up a reason why she can't come along."

—●—

"Mother, that dog is vicious! I don't think you'll ever train him."

"Nonsense, dear, you should have seen your father when I first married him!"

—●—

"Mabel, I hear that you and your husband aren't getting along these days," said the town gossip with a smirk.

"Oh, I wouldn't say that," mused Mabel. "It's true that we had a fight and I stabbed him, but that's as far as it went."

—●—

"Wake up, John," she whispered. "There's a burglar going through your pants pockets."

"For heaven's sake, Ethel, leave me out of it!" he replied sleepily. "You two will just have to fight it out between you."

—●—

"How long have you been married, Mr. Soames?"

"Twenty-odd years, my friend, twenty-odd years!" came the weary reply.

"Why do you say twenty-*odd* years?"

"Just wait till you meet my wife."

—●—

"Why won't you marry me?" demanded the ardent if somewhat conceited suitor. "There can't be anyone else."

"Oh, Henry," came the heartfelt reply, "there must be."

—●—

"Daddy," said little Rose, "what's a financial wizard?"

"Well, darling," replied her old man, "that's a guy who has discovered some magic formula for making more money than his wife can spend."

—●—

An aspiring young actor got his first part in an off-Broadway play. He was terribly excited, and he decided to call home with the good news. "Guess what, Dad!" he shouted happily into the phone. "I got my first part today."

"That's fine, son. What are you playing?"

"I'm going to play the part of a man who's been married for twenty-five years."

"Oh," replied his father. "Well, maybe next time you'll get a speaking part."

—●—

"Mr. Hargrove, I really don't understand this provision in your will," said his puzzled lawyer.

"Which provision is that?"

"The one that stipulates that your wife must remarry before receiving any part of your estate. Why do you insist she remarry?"

"Well," replied Hargrove, "it's a pity for a man to go unmourned. I want somebody to be sorry I died."

—•—

"I want you to follow my husband day and night," demanded Mrs. Finch. "I'm sure there's another woman."

"I understand completely," replied the private eye. "I'll get the goods on her."

"Never mind her. I want a full report on what it is she sees in *him!*"

—•—

"Tell me, Mr. Goldstone," asked the psychiatrist, "do you cheat on your wife?"

"Who else?" said Mr. Goldstone.

—•—

Two friends got to talking during the long ride home. One said, "My wife had a funny dream last night. She dreamed that she was married to a millionaire."

"That's not funny, my friend, that's lucky," replied the second commuter.

"How do you mean 'lucky'?"

"I mean it's lucky you aren't married to my wife. She dreams that in the daytime."

—•—

One member of the local draft board claims he has finally seen everything. A young man insisted he was not eligible for the draft due to defective eyesight, and he brought his wife along to prove the point.

—•—

A group of friends decided to surprise Max with a party to celebrate his twenty-fifth wedding anniversary. The party was going full blast when one of his friends realized that Max had disappeared. He began searching and finally came across Max slumped in a chair in his den.

"What's wrong, old buddy? Is the party too much for you?"

"No, it's not that."

"Then what's wrong, Max?"

"Well, it's like this. When my wife and I had been married for five years, I knew I hated her and that I wanted to kill her. I asked my lawyer what the penalty would be for such a crime, and he assured me that even with time off for good behavior it meant twenty years in jail."

"I don't get it, Max," confessed his friend. "Why should you be sad about not spending twenty years in prison?"

"I can't help but think if I had done it, today I'd be a free man."

—•—

A rather grouchy businessman attended a lecture on married life. He was so taken by some of the lecturer's ideas and so ashamed of himself for being such an insensitive husband that he decided to start making amends that very night. When he arrived home that evening, he presented his wife with a bouquet of roses, told her he was going to take her out to dinner, and then, throwing his arms around her, began nuzzling her neck. "Oh, for heaven's sake!" cried his wife. "This is just too much. First, the baby fell out of his crib, then the washing machine broke down and blew every fuse in the house. And tonight, of all nights, you come home drunk."

—•—

"Boss, can I take tomorrow off?" asked poor, meek Martin Mudd. "My wife wants me to go shopping with her."

"You cannot! What do you think I'm running here—a resort?"

"Thanks, boss. You don't know how much I appreciate this."

—•—

"You can tell me the truth, Doc," said the earnest husband.

"Well," replied the doctor, "then I must tell you that your wife is insane. Her mind is completely gone."

"I'm not really surprised, Doc. After all, she's given me a piece of it every day for the last ten years."

—•—

A modern-day Lewis and Clark exploration team had returned from a two-year exploration of the upper Amazon. Having bravely gone where no men had gone before, they were greeted by members of the press from every nation.

"Tell us, sir," asked a reporter of the first explorer, "what made you go?"

"I had to go," he replied. "I had to meet the challenge, to test my mettle, to meet the unknown, to face hardship, and to ponder the real meaning of life."

"And you, sir," he inquired of the second explorer, "why did you go?"

"You should meet my wife" came the weary reply.

—●—

"You know," said the lovely blonde to her handsome companion, "for months I just couldn't figure out where my husband was spending his evenings."

"What did you do about it?" asked her friend.

"Oh, nothing. I just went home early one night, and *there* he was."

—●—

A henpecked husband began spending more and more time away from home. Night after night he found it necessary to "work late at the office," or at least that's what he told his wife. However, it took only one phone call from his wife to his empty office to undo him. She confronted him furiously, but for once in his life he stood up to her.

"You're absolutely right," he said. "I have been going out with other women. As a matter of fact," he said in his toughest voice, "I have a date tonight. And *you* are going to help me get ready. You know who's going to shine my shoes? You are! And you know who's going to press my pants? You are! And you know who's going to pick out my tie?"

"I certainly do," said his wife. "The undertaker."

—●—

Two co-eds were discussing their boyfriends, "Your fiancé is graduating from medical school this June, isn't he?" asked the first.

"Yes, he is," replied her friend.

"Then I guess you'll be getting married right away."

"Oh, no," the girl replied. "I want him to practice for at least a year first."

—●—

"Darling," sighed the lovely young girl. "Let's get married."

"I don't know," replied the object of her affection. "Who do you suppose would have us?"

MARTIANS

A Martian spaceship crashed into the desert. The Martian pilot and copilot escaped unharmed, but after looking around the desert and sizing up their situation, they were terribly discouraged. "We'll never get back home," moaned the Martian copilot. "Our ship is damaged; our engines are dead. What are we going to do?"

"Now, don't panic," said his commanding officer severely. "We'll put our heads together and find a way. After all, four heads are better than two."

—●—

A Martian landed at a busy cross section in New York City and spent the next two hours crossing the street. He kept going back and forth between the two electric signs that change from "Walk" to "Don't Walk" and then back again. Finally the weary little Martian stopped at one of the poles and threw his arms around it. "Baby," he said, "I really do love you, but you've got to stop being such a nag."

MATING SEASON

A man took his three kids to the zoo one Saturday. When they got to the monkey island, it was empty. Since his children wanted very much to see the monkeys, he found a zoo-keeper and inquired as to the whereabouts of the monkeys. "They are all in the back of the cave," replied the zoo-keeper tactfully. "It's the mating season, you know."

"If we throw some peanuts down to them, do you think they'll come out?" inquired the man.

"I doubt it!" replied the zoo-keeper. "Would you?"

MEMORY

"Doctor, you have simply got to help me. I have a terrible problem."

"Be calm, Mr. Jessup," said the doctor. "Tell me what the trouble is."

"It's just that I can't remember what I have just said."

"When did you first notice it?" asked the doctor.

"Notice what?"

—●—

"My wife has the worst memory in the world," complained Homer.

"That's too bad," said his friend. "It must be awful to live with a wife who forgets everything."

"No," said Homer sadly, "it's awful to live with a wife who *remembers* everything."

MEN

Rosie and Josephine were having a cup of coffee one morning. "What's the matter, Rosie?"

"Well, last night I told my boyfriend I didn't want to see him anymore."

"Really? What did he say to that?"

"Nothing. He just pulled the covers over his head."

—●—

Two old cronies met in a bar. "What's the matter, Fred?" asked the first man. "You look terrible."

"To tell you the truth," replied Fred, "I'm scared. I got a letter from a guy who says he'll kill me if I don't stay away from his wife."

"Well, what are you scared of? All you have to do is stay away from the guy's wife."

"Yeah," said Fred, "I wish it was that easy."

"Well, what's the problem?"

"The problem is," replied Fred grimly, "the guy didn't sign his name."

—●—

Two men at the bowling alley. "I saw Sam Brown the other night," said the first. "He was with his wife. I wouldn't treat a dog like that."

"Oh, what was he doing?" asked his friend.

"He was *kissing* her."

—●—

A woman of the world offered this advice to a naïve young friend. Just remember that a brute is an imperfect animal. Man, alone, is a perfect *beast*.

—●—

A beautiful girl got on a crowded bus one afternoon and eventually found a seat in the rear. When she sat down, her maxi coat fell open, exposing a pair of long, shapely legs and a very brief pair of hot pants. The man sitting across the aisle spent the next fifteen minutes ogling the stylish girl and marveling at his good fortune. She grew more and more uncomfortable under his appreciative gaze and finally hissed, "I can see that you are no gentleman."

"Well," he replied, "I am happy to say that I can see the same about you."

—●—

What makes you think this is a man's world? When a man is born, people ask, "How is his mother doing?" When he marries, all people can say is, "What a lovely bride." And when he finally dies, all people want to know is, "How much did he leave her?"

MESS

An all-girl band was entertaining the troops at a remote army base in Alaska. They had been playing all afternoon and were tired and hungry. At the close of their performance the base commander inquired, "Would you girls like to mess with the enlisted men or the officers tonight?"

"What's the difference?" said one stunning musician. "Just so we get something to eat first."

MICE

Two little mice were sitting on the corner watching all the pretty little girl mice go by. The first little mouse could hardly contain himself. "Wow, look at those legs." "Hey, did you see that dress?" "Get a look at that gorgeous blonde hair." Over and over he cited some favorable point about each new passing beauty. But his companion uttered not a word.

"What's the matter with you?" asked the first little mouse. "You sick or something? Some guys just don't have any appreciation."

"Oh, it isn't that," said the quiet little mouse. "I guess it's just my nature. You see, I'm a titmouse."

MIDWEST

A noted author cabled his agent in New York telling him to cancel the rest of his midwestern speaking tour. The agent called his client intending to soothe his ruffled feathers. "But you don't understand," cried the distressed author. "I don't mind if my audience glances at their watches every now and then. But out here they *shake* them."

MILKMEN

"You know," said one golfing buddy to another, "I hear that Ethel and Fred are getting a divorce."

"You don't say. On what grounds?"

"Well, it seems that Fred found out that Ethel was running around with another man."

"Really? How do you suppose he found out?"

"Fred told me he never suspected a thing until he and Ethel moved from New York to Florida. That's when he noticed that they still had the same milkman."

MODERN SCIENCE

Isn't modern science wonderful? And those scientists don't just worry about inventing a better rocket fuel. They are concerned about the little things, too. Like onions. A whole lab full of scientists are working round the clock to develop an onion that won't make a housewife cry when she peels it. And you can bet that they will, too. After all, they managed to come up with a vitamin-packed, iron-fortified, completely tasteless loaf of bread, didn't they?

—•—

Did you hear about that brand-new deodorant called Invisible? You apply it, and it makes you disappear. Then everyone wonders where that peculiar odor is coming from.

MOTHERS

"All that I am," bragged Pomeroy, the office bore, "I owe to my mother."

"Oh, really?" said one of his co-workers nastily. "Then why not send the old girl a quarter and square the account?"

—•—

Her darling boy had been drafted, and as she watched him pack to leave for boot camp, she offered him some final motherly advice. "Do try to be punctual, my dear—especially in the morning so they won't have to keep your breakfast waiting."

—•—

Mrs. Katz and Mrs. Roth were having a chat one morning. "How's your daughter making out in her new job?" asked Mrs. Roth.

"Well, I'm a little worried about her. She didn't come home until late last night, and she just called to say that she'd be late again tonight."

"She must be working very hard."

"I suppose so," mused her mother. "All she said was that she had made a mistake last night and her boss wanted her to do it again tonight."

—•—

Two women were talking about their children. "My son wanted to become a doctor, but he couldn't stand the sight of blood," moaned the first.

"You think *that's* bad? My son wanted to become a tree surgeon, but he couldn't stand the sight of sap."

—•—

Soon after graduating from college Irma expressed a desire to move into an apartment of her own. Her parents were terribly upset but after many heated discussions finally agreed. However, they would agree on only one condition: Irma would not allow men to visit her in her apartment, because it would worry her mother. So Irma moved out and soon settled down on her own. She made it a habit to call her mother frequently, and during one call Irma described a date she had had the previous evening.

"You didn't invite that young man to your apartment?" asked her suspicious mother.

"Oh, no," replied Irma reassuringly. "I went to his apartment. Now *his* mother can worry."

—●—

A nice young Jewish boy named Fred graduated from the university with honors, so his parents decided to send him to Europe as a graduation present. Three months later Fred was back with his French fiancée. "Mama," he said, "I want you to meet my future wife." Mama wasn't any too pleased by the prospective bride with her fancy clothes and foreign accent, so she lost no time in taking Fred aside.

"My boy, this girl doesn't look like so much to me, you'll excuse my saying so," she said.

"But Mama," protested Fred, "she's a baroness. Doesn't that mean anything to you?"

"Oy," wailed Mama, "you mean she can't have any children?"

MULES

Old Abner was very late getting home to supper. When he finally did arrive, his wife called out to him, "Land sakes, Ab, you sure are late. Did that old wagon break down again?"

"No, Effie," replied the old farmer, "but I found the minister out on the road with a flat tire and offered him a ride. And after he got into our wagon them mules never understood a word I said."

—●—

A man was driving through a small, seemingly deserted town when suddenly he came upon a huge crowd of people gathered in front of the town hall. His curiosity got the best of him, so he parked his car and joined the crowd.

"What's going on?" he inquired of one of the townspeople.

"Jed Blacker's mule kicked his mother-in-law in the head and killed her" was the reply.

"Oh, then this is a memorial service."

"Hell, no, stranger," replied the townsman. "This here's an auction. Every man in town wants to buy that mule."

MUSIC

I went to a nightclub the other night where the music was so bad that a waiter dropped a tray and they gave the band a hand.

—●—

Mr. Hart rushed to the hospital and demanded to see his teen-age son. He was taken to the boy's room and found that his son had a broken leg and was covered with cuts and bruises.

"My God," exclaimed his father, "what happened? Did you have an accident?"

"No, Dad, nothing like that," the boy assured him. "I took my girl home, and we went into her playroom and put on some records and started to dance. Well, her father came home, and he's deaf. He came into the playroom and saw us, but he couldn't hear the music. He threw me out right through their front window."

—●—

Two friends were discussing a mutual friend's miraculous recovery. "It really looked like MacGregor was done for," said one. "His last request was that he hear the bagpipes once more before he went to meet his Maker."

"But I hear he recovered."

"He did. His wife hired a piper to go down to the hospital and play for him, and the very next day he started to improve."

"That's amazing," said the other.

"However, the hospital is being sued."

"What on earth for?" asked his friend.

"After the piper left, five other patients in the ward died."

—●—

"You know," confided a man to his accountant, "my kid's violin lessons were worth a fortune to me."

"Why is that?" asked the accountant.

"Well, for one thing, they enabled me to buy all my neighbor's houses for a song."

—●—

That guy is what you'd call a real music-lover. Why, if he heard a sweet soprano voice coming from the bathroom, he'd put his *ear* to the keyhole.

MUSICIANS

Two musicians were discussing a mutual friend. "It was terrible, just terrible, about Maurice," said the first.

"What happened?"

"He was playing in a concert and his toupee fell into his French horn."

"Yes, I can understand that he would be embarrassed, but is it really so terrible?"

"The accident, no. It was the review all the papers carried that was so awful."

"What review?"

"The one that said that Maurice spent the whole evening blowing his top."

—●—

A new conductor was having a terrible time getting his musicians to show up for rehearsals. He tried everything—threats, cajolery, fines—but nothing worked. Through it all he managed to put together a program that would serve for their first concert. Finally the big day dawned. The conductor appeared at the final preconcert rehearsal, looked over the musicians, and said, "Gentlemen, we have had our differences, but tonight is our first concert together. We will be playing some of the world's greatest music, and I know you will all do your best. Before we start this final rehearsal, I would like to thank Mr. Brunswik, our cymbal-player. He has appeared faithfully at every rehearsal. His devotion inspired me to include the '1812 Overture' in tonight's performance."

"Gee," said Mr. Brunswik, obviously touched. "I wish you hadn't done that."

"But I wanted to do it Your devotion deserves a reward. I selected this piece of music to feature you. You were the only man who attended every rehearsal."

"I always attend rehearsals when I haven't anything better to do," admitted Mr. Brunswik, "but that doesn't mean you can count on me showing up for the concerts."

NAMES

A young intern watched an attractive maternity patient search through a telephone directory without seeming to find whatever she was looking for. "Perhaps I might be able to help," he said with a smile.

"I doubt it," replied the new mother. "I'm trying to find a name for my baby."

"Well, then, I can help," replied the intern. "You see, the hospital supplies each new mother with a booklet that lists every first name and its meaning for both boys and girls. I'd be happy to see that you get one."

"No thanks," replied the girl sadly. "My baby already has a first name."

NATURAL LAW

"Miss Fitzgerald," said the physics professor, "kindly tell the class what happens when a body is immersed in water."

"Well, professor," replied the pretty co-ed, "usually the first thing that happens is the phone rings."

NEIGHBORS

"Well, Mrs. O'Hara," sneered the neighborhood gossip, "I saw your daughter walking down the street at three A.M. this morning. Now *my* daughter was in bed last night at midnight."

"So I heard," replied Mrs. O'Hara, "but my daughter walked home."

NEW ENGLANDERS

New Englanders are notorious for their thrifty ways, but I think one family went too far. They put an ad in yesterday's paper: "For sale—One tombstone, already engraved. Great bargain for family named Hunnicut."

—●—

An old New England fisherman was informed by the Coast Guard that the body of his mother-in-law had been found floating in the bay with a five-pound lobster firmly attached to each of her big toes. The caller inquired, "What shall we do with the body?"

The thrifty old New Englander replied, "Put the lobsters in my trap, and set the old girl out again."

NEW YEAR'S DAY

Have you ever wondered why it's so quiet on New Year's Day? Quite simple, really, when you consider how many wives aren't speaking to their husbands.

NEW YORK

A man walking down Park Avenue stopped and tossed a coin into a blind beggar's cup. Much to his surprise, the beggar took off his dark glasses, looked at the coin, and then put it in his pocket.

"Hey, what's the idea?" said the man. "You're not blind."
"No, but the blind guy hired me to fill in for him on his day off."

NEWLYWEDS

Two newlyweds were determined to check in to a motel without having to endure all the smirks and snide remarks of the clerk and bellboys. So before they arrived at the motel, they pulled over to the side of the road, got out of the car, shook the rice out of their hair, swept it out of the car, removed the Just Married sign from the back of the car, and then got back in, assuring themselves that there was nothing left to give them away. But when they checked in, there was no mistaking them for anything else but honeymooners. The new husband stepped up to the desk and confidently informed the clerk that he and his wife wanted a double bed with a room.

—●—

"Mr. Leroy, tell us," said a member of the press, "to what do you attribute your long life and good health?"

"Well, son, I'll tell you," replied Mr. Leroy on the occasion of his one-hundredth birthday, "I have always tried to remember a piece of advice my father gave to me when I was just a boy."

"What did he say?" asked the reporter.

"My father told me never to try to keep up with the Joneses because they might be newlyweds."

—●—

Two brothers had lived together for many years in a shack way up in the hills. One morning the older brother left for town, and that night when he returned, he brought along his new wife, a buxom young girl at least thirty years his junior. Not too long thereafter his younger brother moved out and left the newlyweds to themselves. The local minister offered to lend the man a hand getting settled in town and began introducing him to the local townspeople.

As they were going from house to house, the minister chanced to say, "A lot of folks think your brother is an old fool, but I admire you, Matt. Not every man would have enough tact to move out of the only home he'd ever known so a newly married couple could start their married life in privacy."

"I appreciate the kind words, preacher," said Matt. "But that ain't why I moved out."

"Then why did you move?" asked the preacher.

"Because," replied Matt, "I never could stand to see a man start a full day's work so late in the day."

"Darling," said the new bride as they drove up to the motel, "let's try to act as if we've been married for years."

"Anything you say, dear," replied the groom, "but do you think you can manage all that luggage?"

"Dear, I'm awfully sorry, but our dinner got a little burned this evening," said the new bride.

"Oh, really? Was there a fire at the delicatessen?"

"Darling," purred the new bridegroom, "remember how you always said that once we were married, my troubles would be your troubles?"

"Of course, I remember, dearest," she replied, "and I meant every word."

"I know you did, my pet. That's why I think you should know that your friend Mary is suing *us* for breach of promise."

"Darling," whispered the young groom on his wedding night, "am I the first man to make love to you?"

"Of course," she replied firmly. "Why do all you men ask the same silly question?"

An innocent young bride went off on a two-week honeymoon; however, she lost no time calling her mother as soon as she returned. "Mom, it was wonderful," she said, sighing, "but one thing bothers me: Just when *do* men sleep?"

It was the eve of their honeymoon, and Clara and George were settled into a cabin in the woods. Clara slipped into a sheer nightgown and crawled into bed, but George seemed to be preparing to sleep on the couch.

"George, darling, what are you doing on the couch? Aren't you going to make love to me?"

"No, dear, not tonight," he replied sadly.

"But why not?" she cried.

"I can't, dear, because it's Lent."

"Oh," sobbed Clara, "that's the most horrible thing I've ever heard. To whom and for how long?"

NIGHTCLUBS

I went to a very exclusive nightclub in Beverly Hills last week. It's so chic they even have a full-time gardener on the staff. Every morning he arrives to water the lawn, the flowers, and the liquor.

NUDISTS

Two men at a nudist colony were watching the world go by. A beautiful girl strolled past on her way to the pool. "Wow!" said the first man to his friend. "Just think how she would look in a bathing suit."

—●—

Two members of a nudist colony were entertaining a weekend guest. Their guest was a rather sophisticated gentleman who did not seem the least uncomfortable in his surroundings. However, his host could see that there was something on his mind.

"Yes," admitted the guest, "I do have one question. It may seem silly, but I've noticed that all the men in this colony are clean-shaven except for Mr. Pringle, and he has a beard down to his knees. Why is that?"

"Quite simple, really," replied his host. "Pringle is the one who goes out for cigarettes."

NURSES

"Tell me, nurse," demanded the irate doctor, "why haven't you kept a detailed chart of this patient's progress?"

"Now, don't worry, Doctor," she said. "I can always show you my diary."

—●—

A student nurse who was not yet familiar with all the hospital slang was unaware that the euphemism in her hospital for "bedpan" was "vase." You can imagine the uproar she caused when one of her patients asked her to bring him a vase in a hurry and she replied, "Sure, if you'll just tell me how big your bouquet is."

—•—

A student nurse answered the phone at the busy nurse's station in a metropolitan hospital. The irate caller demanded to know the condition of one Max Greenburg. The young nurse was very cooperative and checked the patient's chart. In her most professional tone she informed the caller that although Mr. Greenburg had been ill for several months, he had spent a restful night and his condition was improving steadily. Then, as an afterthought, the young nurse inquired as to who was calling.

The relieved caller replied, "This *is* Max Greenburg. I've been here four months, and my doctor won't tell me anything."

NUTS

"I know you are ready to leave the hospital," said the doctor to his patient. "You're sure you are all over the idea that you are an Irish setter?"

"Perfectly sure," replied the patient.

"Well, then, how do you feel?" asked the doctor.

"Perfectly healthy, Doc. Just feel my nose."

—•—

A man entered the psychiatrist's office, sat down in a chair, took a tobacco pouch from his pocket, and began stuffing pipe tobacco into his left ear.

"Well, Mr. Jenkins," said the concerned doctor, "I think you've come to the right place. How can I help you?"

"Have you got a light?"

—•—

"My whole family was sort of strange, Doc," admitted the patient.

"What do you mean by 'strange'?" asked the psychiatrist.

"Well, take my brother. Once when we were kids, we were playing outside. It was his birthday. He tripped and fell down a dry well."

"Well, that certainly is sad," admitted the doctor, "but why do you think it is strange?"

"When we lowered his birthday cake down to him, he didn't even tug on the rope to say thanks."

—●—

"Doctor," gasped a frantic voice on the phone, "come quick. Little Johnny has swallowed my fountain pen."

"I'll be right over," said the doctor. "What are you doing in the meantime?"

"I'm using a ball-point."

—●—

"Now, tell me why you feel that your parents rejected you," said the psychiatrist.

"Well, for one thing, there were all those times when I would come home from school, and they weren't home," said the patient.

"Did it occur to you that they might be out taking a walk or doing the marketing or any number of errands?" said the doctor.

"Yeah, but nobody takes the furniture with them when they go for a walk."

—●—

A man went to his doctor complaining bitterly that he had an eggplant growing out of his left ear. The doctor, needless to say, was amazed to find that his patient did indeed have an eggplant growing out of his ear.

"You must be terribly upset," said the doctor sympathetically.

"You bet I am, Doc," said his patient. "I hate eggplant. I planted radishes."

—●—

The director of a well-known mental hospital decided to resign his post after many years of service. This decision brought the local press out for an interview.

"Tell us, Doctor, what are your plans? Will you resume private practice?"

"Well, I have given it some thought," replied the doctor. "I may go back into private practice, but on the other hand I may become a teakettle."

Two Australians were talking. "What's this I hear about your uncle being in a mental institution?" said the first.

"Terrible thing," replied the second Aussie. "He bought himself a new boomerang and went crazy trying to throw the old one away."

One inmate in a mental institution was watching another inmate who had a rod and reel and was fishing in an empty bucket. Thinking to make a little conversation, the first inmate said, "How many did you catch today?"

The other inmate replied, "No wonder you're in a mental institution. You can't catch fish out of an empty bucket."

"Tell me a little about your family," said the psychiatrist.

"Well, I think there was something peculiar about my sister," admitted the patient.

"What do you mean?"

"For one thing, she thought she was a chicken. She would run around the house clucking and scratching and trying to build a nest."

"That does sound peculiar," admitted the psychiatrist. "What did your parents do about her condition?"

"Nothing, Doctor. We were a poor family, and besides, we needed the eggs."

"Doctor, I want you to start treating my son immediately."

"Just what seems to be the problem?"

"He spends all his time making mudpies."

"Well, that's not so bad. At a certain age it is even quite normal."

"Well, I don't think it's normal, and neither does his wife."

"Doctor, you've got to do something about my husband."

"What seems to be the problem?"

"He's convinced that he's a refrigerator."

"That's terrible."

"You're telling me!" snapped the wife. "He sleeps with his mouth open, and the light keeps me awake all night."

—●—

A man rushed into a psychiatrist's office and said, "Doctor, you've got to help me. It's my brother. He thinks he's a cocker spaniel."

"Why, that's terrible," said the doctor. "How long has he been suffering from this delusion?"

"About six months," replied the man. "Ever since he stopped believing he was a Saint Bernard."

"What made him change his mind?" inquired the doctor.

"He lost his liquor license."

—●—

"Doctor, you've got to help me. My husband thinks he's a dog."

"That sounds serious. What kind of a dog?"

"A dachshund."

"That *is* serious. How long has this been going on?"

"Ever since he was a puppy."

—●—

A woman called a psychiatrist on the phone and cried, "Doctor, you've got to help me. My husband is driving me crazy. He keeps insisting that he's Moses."

"That sounds serious," replied the psychiatrist. "I think you should bring him to my office tomorrow."

"Oh, I will," she replied, "but in the meantime how do I keep him from parting the water every time I try to take a bath?"

—●—

Two old friends met in a bar one evening.

"What's new, Fred?"

"Well, for one thing I have a daffodil growing out of my head."

"That's impossible!" exclaimed his friend, thinking Fred had had one too many.

"It's true," insisted Fred.

To prove his point, he took off his hat, and sure enough, a daffodil was growing out of his head.

"Good God, you're right," agreed his friend. "So what *else* is new?"

OPERA

Two members of an opera company were discussing the star's understudy. "You know," said one, "that girl is really determined to be heard. Why, she's always breaking into song."

"Well," replied the other, "she wouldn't have to *break* in if she could find a key."

An aging diva was trying to impress the Met's newest soprano. "I'll have you know that my voice was insured for one hundred thousand dollars," she said haughtily.

"Really?" purred the younger woman. "Whatever did you do with all that money?"

OPTIMISTS

Optimism can be a wonderful thing unless it is carried to extremes. A fellow named Fred was such an optimist that he very nearly lost every friend he had. No matter what kind of a hard-luck story anyone told Fred, he was never sympathetic. He would listen patiently but always replied optimistically, "Yes, I understand, but it *could* have been worse." Thinking to cure him of this aggravating habit, one of his few remaining friends decided to tell him a story so horrifying, so terrible, that there couldn't possibly be anything worse.

"Fred, did you hear about George?" he asked.

"No, what happened?"

"Well, last night George came home and found his wife in bed with his best friend. He took out a revolver and shot them both, and then he committed suicide."

"Well," mused Fred, "it *could* have been worse."

"For heaven's sake, Fred!" exploded his friend. "Two murders and a suicide? How on earth could it be any worse?"

"I'll tell you how," replied Fred. "If it had happened the night before last, I'd be a dead man today."

I know a guy who is such an optimist that every year on his wedding anniversary he goes down to city hall to see if his marriage license has expired.

Pessimist to optimist: "I'm broke, the bank is about to foreclose on my house, I owe every store in town, and I don't have a cent coming in. What do I have to be thankful for?"

Optimist to pessimist: "Be thankful you aren't one of your creditors."

OVERWEIGHT

An overweight lady happened to meet a woman of her acquaintance who had recently dieted off about twenty pounds. Feeling a little jealous of her friend's newly acquired svelte figure, the plump lady said spitefully, "My goodness, Gloria, you look as though you've been through a famine."

"You think so?" said Gloria with a snide smile. "You look as if you might have caused one."

Why do you suppose fat people are so good-natured?
Probably because they can't fight *or* run.

A very fat lady struggled to get up the steps and onto a crosstown bus, but no matter how she tried, she couldn't quite make it. Finally she turned to a man waiting patiently behind her and said, "If you were half a man, you would help me onto this bus."

The man thought for a moment and replied, "Yes, but if you were half a lady, you wouldn't need any help."

A poor, hapless tramp stopped a very fat lady and asked her for a quarter. "Please, lady," he said. "I ain't eaten in three days."

"I wish I had your willpower," she replied and continued on her way.

PARAKEETS

A man went back to the pet shop where he had purchased a parakeet several weeks before and said, "You have a hell of a nerve selling me that talking parakeet." The owner was rather surprised, since he remembered this particular customer because he had been so insistent about buying a talking parakeet.

"What's the matter?" asked the owner. "Won't the bird talk?"

"Oh, he talks all right," replied the bird's owner, "but how would you like to live with a sarcastic parakeet?"

"I don't think I quite understand," replied the owner of the pet store.

"Well," said the man, "when I took that bird home, every morning for a solid week I would stand outside his cage and say, 'Can you talk?' and for a solid week I got no answer. So one morning I was really disgusted, and I said, 'What's the matter, stupid? Can't you talk?' And that parakeet looked at me and said, 'I can talk, all right, but can you *fly*'?"

PARENTHOOD

"Honey," said the new bride, "I know that something is bothering you. I can tell. I want you to confide in me. After all, we promised to share everything whether it is for better or for worse."

"But, darling," replied her husband, "this time it's different."

"Nonsense," she replied. "Together we can face anything. Now, I want you to tell me what *our* problem is."

"Okay, if you insist," said the husband. "*We* have just become the father of an illegitimate child."

—●—

It was a very nervous father-to-be pacing back and forth in the waiting room awaiting the doctor's arrival. After what seemed like an eternity the door opened, and Dr. Samuels entered the room.

"Congratulations, Mr. Lewis," said the doctor while vigorously shaking his hand. "You will be happy to know that your wife has just given birth to six perfectly healthy baby girls."

Visibly shaken by the news, Mr. Lewis needed several minutes to compose himself. "Well, Doc," he was finally heard to say. "When we were first married, I used to call Helen my little pussycat. I guess she figured it was all right to go and have a litter."

PARROTS

A little old lady returned to the pet shop where she had just recently purchased a parrot. "Now, listen here," she said angrily to the owner. "That parrot swears like a drunken sailor. He's humiliated me in front of my friends, called the minister filthy names the other day while he was having tea with me, and then kept me up half the night with his foul mouth."

"Well, lady," said the owner sympathetically, "you have one consolation. Sure, he swears like a drunken sailor, but he doesn't drink, he doesn't gamble, and he doesn't run around with other parrots."

—●—

A widower whose children had all grown up, gotten married, and moved away was extremely fond of his pet parrot. He lavished all of his affection on the bird, and he was terribly upset when the parrot grew listless and disinterested in everything and everyone. Finally the man took his beloved bird to a vet.

"Don't worry," the doctor said. "It is only that the bird is lonely for one of its own kind. It's the mating season, and this parrot needs a mate."

The man was greatly relieved, and he set about the task of finding a female parrot who would be good enough for his precious pet. He finally found a beautiful parrot. She had a terrific figure, and her plumage was magnificent. She cost one hundred dollars, but nothing was too good for his bird. He took her home, introduced her to his parrot, slipped her into the cage, and withdrew quietly to allow nature to take its course. About fifteen minutes later he heard a terrible commotion. Rushing into the room, he found the lady parrot on the floor of the cage while his parrot was tearing out her feathers with his beak.

"What are you doing?" cried the man in alarm.

"Listen," said his parrot, "you paid one hundred dollars for this dame, and for that much I want her naked."

PEARLS OF WISDOM

When asked how he managed to make his fortune, Mr. Bigelow replied, "I always kept this in mind: A man can always do more than he thinks he can and generally does less than he thinks he did."

PERFUME

A little girl, about ten years old, went to a big department store and made her way up to the perfume counter. "Excuse me, mister," she said to the salesman, "I'd like to buy some perfume."

"Certainly, mademoiselle," replied the salesman. "We have something here called One Night of Lust. Would you like to try that?"

"No," replied the child, "that doesn't sound like me."

"Well, how about Flaming Desire?"

"I don't think so," replied the child.

"Well, how about our best-seller, Burning Kiss of Venus?"

"Look, mister," said the little girl, "haven't you got something for beginners?"

PICNICS

"Oh, Henry," cried the sweet young thing, "what a perfect spot for a picnic."

"I guess so," replied Henry. "After all, fifty million ants can't be wrong."

POINT OF VIEW

Two white rats were chatting through the bars of their laboratory cages. "Tell me," said the first white rat, "how are you getting along with Dr. Smith?"

"Just fine," replied the second rat. "It took awhile, but I've finally got him trained. Now whenever I ring the bell, he brings me my dinner."

POLITICS

Commissar Petrovich had come all the way from Moscow to speak to the workers during the opening ceremonies of the state's brand-new tractor factory. After four hours of incredibly dull rhetoric lauding the glories of the state he was still going strong. The audience, however, was getting weaker by the minute. Suddenly he shouted to the guards, "Arrest that man! The one in the eighth seat in the third row. He is a spy." The guards rushed forward, seized the man, and carried him off. Hours later he confessed that he was indeed a spy. Later that evening the commissar was traveling back to Moscow when a young captain in his entourage asked him how he had known that that man was a spy when he was no different in appearance from any of the other workers in the hall. "Simple, my boy," replied Petrovitch. "The enemy never sleeps!"

That was some campaign we just had. The Republicans told us the Democrats were crooks. The Democrats told us the Republicans were crooks. It's probably one of the first times in history that two opposing political parties could disagree with each other and still *both* be right.

"Tell me, Senator, strictly off the record, what do you consider the object of legislation?"
"I feel that the object of legislation is to achieve the greatest good for the greatest number."
"And what do you consider the greatest number?"
"Number one, my friend, number one."

An old campaigner was overheard at a recent political rally. After hours of listening to a series of candidates state precisely where they stood, the old man snorted to one of his aides, "We might all be better off if we knew which direction they'll be going once they decide to stop standing and start *moving*."

A well-known writer spent two years traveling with a famous political figure. It took him another two years to assemble his notes, transcribe his tapes, and work the whole thing into a comprehensive character study of a man who might very well become President of the United States one day. The book was highly acclaimed, as well it should have been, but the author has been frustrated ever since. He claims that ever since the book has been out, people keep telling him how much they enjoyed reading it, but they always have one question that really throws him: They all want to know what that famous political figure "is *really* like."

POLLS

A poll-taker placed a call to the Wilkins residence. "Good evening, sir," he said when Mr. Wilkins answered the phone. "I'd like to ask you a few questions about the television programs you watch."

"Go right ahead," said Mr. Wilkins.

"Do you have your television set on right now?"

"Yes, I do."

"Are any other members of your family there with you?"

"Yes, my wife is here."

"What are you listening to?" asked the poll-taker.

"My wife," replied Mr. Wilkins wearily.

POLLUTION

Two men were making their way uptown one hot afternoon. The heat was a minor annoyance compared with the bus and truck fumes which rose noxiously around them. "You know," said one, "I read somewhere that the earth is the only planet in this solar system capable of supporting life."

"No kidding," his friend replied as he gazed up at the smoggy skyline. "What makes them think so?"

POLYGAMY

"Daddy, what is polygamy?"

"Polygamy is a situation in which a man can have more than one wife."

"Okay. So what do you call a situation in which a man can have only one wife?"

"Monotony, my son, monotony."

—●—

"Daddy, why can't a man have more than one wife?"

"Because, my boy, laws are made to protect those who are incapable of protecting themselves."

PRAYERS

A little boy was mumbling his prayers one evening when his mother said, "Speak up, Mike. I can't hear you."

"That's okay, Mom. I wasn't talking to you."

—●—

Mrs. Green was always nagging little Willie about his behavior in church. "And for another thing," she said during one tirade, "how many times do I have to tell you that we keep our eyes closed while we are praying in church!"

"But, Mama," said little Will, "how do *you* know I don't?"

—●—

A man decided to take his vacation in Africa, so he made arrangements to go on a safari. He bought some boots, a bush jacket, and a gun and decided that he was all set to be a big-game hunter. He had been in the jungle for less than an hour when he came across a huge lion sitting peacefully in the grass. He raised his gun, took aim, fired, and missed by a mile. The lion got up and took off after the mighty hunter. The man ran and ran, but it was no use. Knowing he couldn't outrun the king of the jungle, he fell to his knees and started praying. Strangely enough, the lion stopped dead in his tracks and fell to his knees.

"Are you praying, too?" asked the man incredulously.

"No," replied the lion, "I am saying grace."

PRISONS

A prison official was checking some records one day when he noticed that a particular prisoner never had a single visitor since the day he arrived. This really bothered the warden, and finally he sent for the prisoner.

"It has been brought to my attention," said the warden, "that you have never had a single visitor since the day you were brought in. Have you no family, no friends? Isn't there anyone at all you might like to see?"

"Warden," said the prisoner, "I appreciate your concern, but don't worry about it. All of my family and friends are in here, too."

—●—

While all this controversy rages about our prison system, some prison officials are still trying to make their prison more cheerful and homey. But I know one warden who is going too far. He wanted his wife to make slipcovers for the electric chair.

—●—

A man who had been the warden of the same penitentiary for nearly twenty years decided to do something to celebrate his anniversary. He put a suggestion box in the exercise yard, and each prisoner was to vote for the kind of party he wanted. It was unanimous. Every prisoner in the place voted for "Open House."

—●—

The warden answered his phone and said, "No, I'm terribly sorry, but you must have the wrong name. There is no one here by that number."

PROPAGATION

The long voyage was finally over. Noah set down the ramp and proceeded to usher the animals off, two by two. Each time a pair left the ark he would say the same thing: "God bless you. Now go forth and multiply." It was quite a job, but he finally got the ark emptied out, or so he thought, until he came across a pair of snakes coiled up in a corner.

"Well, what are you two waiting for?" he asked. "God bless you. Now go forth and multiply."

"That's the problem," said one of the snakes. "We're adders."

PSYCHIATRISTS

"You know, Doctor," said the prisoner to the gorgeous prison psychiatrist, "I have this mad urge to crush you in my arms."

"Well," she said as she cast an eye over the prisoner's handsome physique, "*now* you're talking sense."

—●—

A father who was concerned about his young son's strange behavior took the boy to a psychiatrist. The doctor proceeded to ask the boy a few questions.

"Tell me, how many wheels does a car have?"

"Four," the boy replied.

"Tell me what a cow has four of that a woman has only two of."

"Legs," the boy answered.

"And what does your father have that your mother likes the most?"

"Money" was the lad's prompt reply.

The doctor turned to the boy's father and said, "You have nothing to worry about. He's just fine and very smart."

The boy's father nodded in agreement and said, "He sure is, Doc. I missed the last two questions myself."

—●—

As soon as the beautiful blonde was admitted to her psychiatrist's office the doctor leaped up, charged across the room, tore off her clothes, threw her down on the couch, and attacked her. A few minutes later he said, "Now that takes care of *my* problem. What's *yours?*"

—•—

After six years of analysis the patient was ready to face the world alone—or at least without the aid of her analyst. "Doctor," she said, "you've done so much for me. Would you do just one more little thing?"

"If I can, my dear," he replied.

"I owe you so much it would make me very happy if you would let me kiss you good-bye."

"Now, my dear, you know that isn't possible," he replied. "Why, I shouldn't even be here on the couch with you."

—•—

A man walked into a bar, ordered a double scotch, drank half of it, and threw the rest in the bartender's face. He then apologized profusely and confessed that this peculiarity of his was getting out of hand and that he was terribly embarrassed by it. The bartender gave him the name of a good psychiatrist, and the man was not seen for several months. Then one night he reappeared, ordered his double scotch, drank half of it, and tossed the rest of it into the bartender's face.

"I see that you didn't go to that doctor I recommended," said the bartender.

"Oh, but I did."

"Well, he doesn't seem to be doing you much good."

"That's where you're wrong. He's done me a world of good."

"But you still threw half your drink in my face."

"I know, but it doesn't embarrass me anymore."

—•—

A man went into a store to buy his wife a gift. When he received the package from the clerk, he started to leave but then turned suddenly and slapped the clerk across the face. No sooner had he done it than the man began to apologize profusely. The clerk was naturally taken aback, but he could not doubt the sincerity of the man's apologies. "Perhaps," suggested the sympathetic clerk, "you ought to see a psychiatrist." A few months later the man reappeared at the store. He made a purchase but made no attempt to do the clerk any harm.

"I took your advice, young man. I went to see a psychiatrist."

"How did he cure you?" inquired the clerk.

"Well," replied the man, "right after I paid him for my first visit I slapped him in the face."

"Then what happened?"

"He slapped me back."

—●—

Two psychiatrists met in an elevator. "What's new?" asked one.

"I have these tiny, invisible creatures crawling all over me," said the other.

"Well," said the first, "for heaven's sake, don't get any on me."

—●—

Psychiatrist: "Do you find that you have trouble making up your mind?"

Patient: "Well, yes . . . and no. . . ."

—●—

"Miss Nolan," said the doctor with a smile, "I think this will be your last visit."

"Oh, Doctor," she said anxiously, "do you really think my kleptomania is cured?"

"Yes, I do," replied her doctor reassuringly. "You haven't stolen a thing in the last six months."

"How can I ever repay you?" said the grateful patient.

"Don't give it another thought," said the doctor. "My fee has been paid by your fiancé, and now that you're cured, I'm sure you two will have every chance at happiness."

"Yes, but are you sure that there is nothing that I can do for you personally?"

"No," replied the doctor, "not for me, but if you should suffer a relapse, you might pick up a nice transistor radio for my son."

—●—

Two colleagues were discussing a patient. "I was having great success with Mr. Green," said the first doctor. "When he first came to me, he was suffering from a massive inferiority complex. And it was all due to his size."

"How did you treat this patient?" inquired the second doctor.

"I started out with intensive analysis and then group therapy. I convinced him that many of the world's greatest leaders were men of small physical stature. I really hated to lose Mr. Green."

"What do you mean?" inquired his colleague. "How did you lose him?"

"A terrible accident," replied the physician. "A pussycat ate him."

—●—

"Doctor, I don't know why I'm here. My wife insisted that I talk to you because she thinks there's something wrong with me."

"What makes her think that?" inquired the doctor.

"I don't know," admitted the patient, "except she sort of resents the way I love pancakes."

"You mean your wife resents your love for pancakes? That's ridiculous," said the doctor. "I love pancakes, too."

"No kidding, Doc? Why don't you come over to my house this evening. I have a whole basement full of them."

—●—

Two call girls were discussing their analysts.

"My doctor is wonderful," said the first. "I used to have these terrible nightmares that men would seduce me and then offer me two dollars for my services."

"Gee," replied her friend sympathetically, "that must have been terrible. Was he able to cure you?"

"He sure was," replied the first enthusiastically. "Now when I have that dream, there isn't a man who doesn't offer me at least two hundred dollars."

PUBLIC SPEAKING

This introduction nearly broke up a meeting. The emcee announced, "Mr. Perkins is our only speaker this evening. The rest of the program is strictly entertainment."

—●—

During a very long, very dull speech one of the members of the audience nudged her neighbor and asked in a whisper, "What follows this speaker?"

"Tomorrow" came the weary reply.

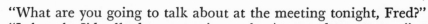

"What are you going to talk about at the meeting tonight, Fred?"

"I thought I'd talk about my trip up the Amazon last summer."

"But you've never been up the Amazon," exclaimed his friend.

"Don't worry about a thing," he replied. "Neither has my audience."

—●—

A politician was making a tour of a penitentiary in his home state. While inspecting the dining room he was called upon by the inmates to make a speech. He began by saying, "Fellow Republicans," but realized instantly that that was hardly a boost for his party. He began again. "Fellow citizens," but once again he knew he had erred. Prisoners relinquish their rights as citizens. However, it was his third start that got the biggest laugh. "My *friends*," he said, "I'm so glad to see you all assembled here."

—●—

Tom Kirby was asked to give a speech to his lodge. After some consideration he decided to speak about sex and marriage. However, fearful of his wife's reaction, he told her that he was going to speak about air travel. A few days after her husband's speech Mrs. Kirby happened to be in the market when she met a woman whose husband belonged to the same lodge.

"That was quite a speech your husband made the other night," said the woman enthusiastically. "He must be an expert."

"Oh, no," replied Mrs. Kirby. "He's only tried it twice. The first time he lost his bag, and the second time he got sick to his stomach."

—●—

What did the circus manager say to the Human Cannon Ball when he decided to quit?

"You can't quit. I'll never find another man of your caliber."

—●—

What happens when you drop a piano into a coal mine?
You get A-flat minor.

—•—

Two show girls were discussing an extremely successful mutual acquaintance. "Tell me," said the first, "how did Sally get started?"
"By being Miss Softdrink," replied her friend.
"You mean by winning a beauty contest?"
"No, by going out with anybody from seven up."

PUTDOWNS

"And what does your husband do?" asked one snobbish matron of the woman seated opposite her at dinner.
"He makes his living with a pen" was her reply.
"Oh, then he's a writer," said the matron solicitously.
"No," replied the other woman, "he raises pigs."

—•—

An old windbag was boring his dinner guests with stories of his adventures hunting big game. After an interminable dinner they went into the library for brandy. There on the floor was a beautiful bearskin rug. "I shot that bear up in Canada," boasted their host. He then launched into forty-five minutes on how he had set up the expedition, hiked through the wilds, tracked the bear for three days, and then finally brought him down with a single shot. "I knew," he concluded, "when I came face to face with that bear, that it was him or me."
"I'm certainly glad it was him, old boy," interjected one of his guests. "He makes a much better rug."

—•—

The town gossip confronted young Mrs. Willoughby in the supermarket. "Tell me, my dear," she inquired of the bulging Mrs. Willoughby, "are you going to have a baby?"
"Oh, no," replied the young matron, "I'm just carrying this for a friend."

—•—

A flashy sports car roared to a stop at a corner where a very attractive girl was waiting for a bus. "I'm going south," said the driver invitingly.

"Wonderful," replied the girl. "Bring me back a grapefruit."

RELIGION

Three young, ambitious rabbis were bragging about how progressive they were. "My congregation is so advanced that we serve ham sandwiches at all our social functions," said the first.

"That's nothing," said the second. "My congregation just built a new synagogue and had the architect put ashtrays in all the pews."

"You guys don't know from progressive until you've seen my congregation," bragged the third rabbi. "We're so reformed that we close for the Jewish holidays."

—●—

Two skid-row bums were talking about a sermon they had heard. "You know," said the first, "those preachers lie."

"What do you mean?"

"Well, they all say the same thing, don't they? They all say you will reap what you sow."

"So what makes you think that's a lie?"

"Is this what you call reaping booze and dames?"

—●—

I think it's important that people of all faiths learn to understand one another. The rabbi of my synagogue is working in an exchange program. Every few weeks he goes to a church of some Christian denomination to speak. Last week he spoke at a Catholic church. The topic of his talk was religious holidays. He told the members of the parish about Yom Kippur, the Day of Atonement. They understood just what he was talking about as soon as he told them it was sort of an Instant Lent.

—●—

"Tell me, Deacon Smith, how long do you usually sleep on Sunday mornings?" inquired the new minister's wife.

"Well, ma'am," he replied, "that depends."

"Depends on what?" she asked.

"On the length of the sermon, ma'am."

—●—

Little Johnny was the son of the local minister. One day his teacher was asking the class what they wanted to be when they grew up.

When it was his turn to answer, he replied, "I want to be a minister just like my father."

The teacher was impressed with his determination, and so she asked him why he wanted to be a preacher.

"Well," he said thoughtfully, "since I have to go to church on Sunday anyway, I figure it would be more interesting to be the guy who stands up and yells than the one who has to sit down and listen."

—●—

"I can't marry him, Mom," moaned Sue.

"Why not, dear? I thought you loved Jerry."

"I do love him, but it will never work."

"Why not?"

"Well, because he's an atheist, and I'm an agnostic."

"But what's the problem?"

"We're already fighting about which religion we *won't* bring our kids up in."

—●—

"Sinners!" shouted the evangelist accusingly at the tent full of true believers. "You are all sinners. Every one of you has something on his conscience, and one sin is just as bad as another. Stealing is as bad as lying. Isn't that so, Brother William?"

Brother William nodded his agreement.

"And adultery is just as bad as murder. Ain't that right, Sister Rose?"

"Can't rightly say, preacher," replied Sister Rose. "I never killed nobody."

RESTAURANTS

The manager at one of New York best-known restaurants was overheard giving this pep talk to his waitresses. "Okay, girls. I want you to really pour it on today. Give it all you've got. Fix your hair. Put on a little extra makeup, and give every customer a great big smile."

"What's up, boss?" asked one of the girls. "Is the owner coming in?"

"No," the manager assured her, "nothing like that. It's just that the meat is tough today."

—•—

Two friends stopped for tea one afternoon. The first gentleman told the waiter that he wanted a cup of tea, very weak, with a piece of lemon. The other man told the waiter that he wanted a cup of tea, very strong, no lemon, but to make sure that the cup was absolutely clean. A few minutes later the waiter was back with a tray. "Now," he said, "which one of you gets the clean cup?"

—•—

A salesman found himself alone in a strange town on his birthday. He was feeling pretty sorry for himself as he stopped in at a local coffee shop for some breakfast. When the waitress asked him what he wanted, he replied, "Two fried eggs and a kind word." She returned with the eggs, and he asked bitterly, "What happened to my kind word?"

She thought for a minute and then leaned over and whispered, "Don't eat the eggs."

—•—

The waiter brought a bowl of soup to his customer, but the man refused to eat it. There was, he insisted, a fly in the soup. So the waiter brought him another bowl of soup. This, too, proved inedible because there appeared to be a hair in the soup. So the patient waiter brought a third bowl of soup to the table. The customer again insisted that he was unable to eat the soup.

"What do you mean you can't eat the soup?" demanded the enraged waiter. "What's wrong with it?"

"Nothing's wrong with it," admitted the customer, "but I can't eat it."

"Why not?"

"Because I don't have a spoon."

—•—

A man went into a restaurant and ordered a cup of coffee without any cream. A few minutes later the waitress reappeared and said,

"We're all out of cream, sir. Would you mind taking your coffee without milk?"

Nobody can complain like my wife. The other day she told me she ate in a restaurant where the food was pure poison. And such small portions, too!

REVENGE

Two old men were sitting peacefully in a canoe out in the middle of the lake. It was a beautiful sunny day, a perfect day for fishing. Suddenly the serene atmosphere was broken. A tourist came roaring out onto the lake in a high-powered speedboat. He went back and forth, up and down, and finally around in a circle before stopping about twenty feet away from the little canoe. The two old men were rocked violently in his wake and very nearly capsized. The tourist proceeded to drop a line over the side, but he had scared all the fish away. In a few minutes he grew impatient and decided to leave. He stood up and turned toward the engine, but he got his foot caught and fell out of the boat. As he surfaced, he cried, "Help, help. I can't swim."

One of the old-timers in the canoe gave him a smile and replied, "Neither can I, son, but I ain't makin' a fuss about it."

Two old Jewish men had hated each other for as long as anyone could remember. No one knew what had started the feud, but there were no two people who hated each other more in all the garment center, possibly in the whole city of New York, and maybe even in the whole world. One morning one of these two men was having coffee in a restaurant with his son, when who should appear but the very man he loathed.

"You know, my son," he said in a voice just loud enough to be overheard by his enemy, "last night I had a very strange dream. I dreamed I was visited by an angel of God, and this angel offered to grant me one wish—anything I wanted, anything in the world, just as long as my worst enemy could have the same thing, only double."

"Gee, Dad," said his son, "what on earth did you wish for?"

"My boy," replied his father in a clear voice his enemy could not help but hear, "I wished that I was blind in *one* eye."

A man was bitten by a dog, and a few days later his doctor told him that the lab tests were positive, that the dog had rabies, and that he, too, was infected. The man pulled out a notebook and began writing furiously.

"Now, take it easy," said the doctor. "No need to start writing your will. You'll pull through."

"Will, hell," snapped the patient. "This is a list of the people I'm going to bite."

THE REVOLUTION

"Come the revolution every man will have a car of his own."

"I'd really like to have a car of my own."

"Come the revolution every man will have a good job."

"I'd really feel great if I had a good job."

"Come the revolution every man will be able to retire and not have to worry about where his next meal is coming from."

"That would really make me feel secure."

"Come the revolution every man will be able to eat pheasant at every meal."

"But I don't like pheasant."

"Come the revolution you'll *like* pheasant."

RIGHT MIND

A man was consoling his friend on the loss of his wealthy ninety-eight-year-old uncle. "Tell me," he said, "was your uncle in his right mind up to the very last?"

"I really don't know" was the reply. "They don't read the will until next week."

RIVALS

A Harvard graduate fell into conversation with a Yale man one evening on a train. "I hear that Harvard is graduating a horse this term. I think that's amazing."

"And what is so amazing about it?" snarled the Harvard grad.

"That this year they're graduating the *entire* horse."

ROMANCE

"Now that I've told you all about my past I guess you won't want to marry me," said John sadly.

"Of course, I want to marry you," said Lou.

"I guess I can live down my past if you'll help me."

"I will not!" she snapped. "But I'll sure try to help you live up to it."

—•—

"What's the matter, Dave?" inquired his friend. "Your girl giving you trouble again?"

"Not exactly," he replied. "It's just that last night when I went to pick her up, her father cornered me in the living room and demanded to know what my intentions were toward his daughter."

"That can be pretty rough," sympathized his friend. "What did you do?"

"Nothing. Just then my girl called down, 'Forget it, Pa, he ain't the one.' "

—•—

Abner was very shy, so it took him quite a while to ask Sue for a date. He finally did, and they went off on horseback to the barn dance. On the way home they stopped to rest the horses.

The two horses began nuzzling each other affectionately, and Abner said wistfully, "Now, that's what I'd like to do."

"Go ahead," replied Sue. "It's your horse."

—•—

A couple of modern-day young people were discussing marriage.

"I have considered the matter carefully," said the young man, "and it seems to me that we should marry."

"What makes you so sure we are suited to each other?" inquired the young lady.

"It's really quite simple," he replied. "Opposites attract. You are fair, and I am dark. You are small and delicately made; I am tall and sturdy. You are cheerful and active; I am more sober and deliberate in my actions. We are, in fact, perfect opposites and therefore should marry."

"What you say is true," admitted the object of his affection, "but we are alike in the one way that makes our marriage an impossibility."

"And what way is that?" he asked.

"I couldn't earn a living, either."

—•—

"How are things between you and Sally?" inquired a friend of young Bill's.

"I think I'm making progress," said Bill.

"You mean she's been giving you some encouragement?" inquired his friend.

"In a way," said Bill. "Last night she said that she had said No for the last time."

—●—

After an evening of eluding her date's amorous advances Lillian was ready to give up and go home.

"Now, you listen to me," she said firmly. "This is positively the last time I am going to say No."

"Wonderful," said her date as he resumed his attack. "Now maybe we can get somewhere."

—●—

A would-be Don Juan and his new girl friend were parked in a secluded spot out in the woods. He advanced; she retreated.

"Be patient," she said. "You must give me time."

"Just tell me how much time, darling," he whispered. "A day, a week?"

"How about until the moon gets behind those clouds?"

—●—

You've all heard the old expression "Two's company, but three's a crowd." Well, in this day and age when two's company, three is often the result.

—●—

I was up on Lovers Lane the other night when a puzzling thought occurred to me. I've always thought that sex was a driving force in man's life, but if that's so, I wonder why so much of it is parked.

—●—

After an evening of dinner, the theater, dancing, and a midnight supper the eager playboy made his move. "Tell me, Doris," he said, breathing gently in his date's ear, "how do you feel about making love?"

"I'll have you know," snapped his date angrily, "that that is *my* business!"

"Oh, I see," replied the playboy nastily, "a professional."

—●—

I overheard this conversation in a very chic restaurant the other night.

"I am a man of few words," said the handsome young man. "Will you, or won't you?"

"Yes, I will," replied his lovely companion. "Your apartment or mine?"

"Look," he snarled, "if we're going to have a big discussion, let's forget the whole thing."

—●—

"My girl is sure the practical type," said one middle-aged Romeo to another. "I finally found the key to her heart. It's the ignition key to a brand-new Rolls Royce."

—●—

Hilda had been dating Herman for over a year when her father finally demanded, "What are his intentions?"

"Well, Papa," replied the blushing girl, "I really don't know. You see, he keeps me pretty much in the dark."

—●—

"Before we get married," said the earnest young man to his bride-to-be, "I want to confess the affairs I've had in the past."

"But, darling," protested his beloved, "you confessed everything only last week."

"I know," he replied honestly. "But that was *last* week."

—●—

A man-about-town found himself the defendant in a paternity suit. He declared himself innocent, but his reputation seemed to be working against him. At one point in the trial the judge demanded, "Tell me, did you ever sleep with this woman?"

"No, your honor," replied the playboy without a moment's hesitation, "not a wink."

—●—

Sometimes these talk-show hosts get more than they bargain for. One emcee offered a lady in his audience a hundred dollars if she would tell him the name of the first man.

"Listen," she replied, "that I wouldn't tell you for a million."

SALESMANSHIP

"Just remember this, my boy," said the sales manager to his newest trainee, "and you will be a great success: Always be sincere, whether you mean it or not."

—●—

One real-estate broker in our town is bound to be a success. The other day his phone rang. It was obviously a wrong number, since the woman calling wanted to know if he sold maternity clothes. "No, madam," was his quick reply, "but can I interest you in a larger house?"

SARCASM

A renowned bridge expert was lecturing at a ladies' club. After his lecture he was in the habit of holding a brief question-and-answer period. A rather overbearing member of the club rose and managed to monopolize the discussion with a description of a hand she had been dealt at her bridge club a few weeks before. When she finally finished her tirade, she asked coyly, "How would you have played that hand, Mr. Brainthwaite?"

"Under an assumed name, madam."

—●—

Two old biddies were discussing a mutual acquaintance. "You'll have to admit that Bertha is very kind to her inferiors," said the first.

"And well she should be," said the other, "considering the trouble she has to go through to find them."

SCOTSMEN

A Scotsman had a very bad toothache. He nursed it along for several weeks, but it grew steadily worse, and finally the thrifty Scot was in such pain he broke down and went to a dentist.

"Doctor," said MacGregor, "how much will you charge to pull this tooth?"

The dentist looked in his mouth and said, "That tooth is infected. It will cost you ten dollars to have it taken out."

"Ten dollars!" roared the miserable MacGregor. "That's robbery. Ten dollars for a minute's work. You're a thief, not a doctor."

"Well," replied the dentist, "if you like, I can extract it very slowly."

—•—

A Scotsman named McDuff went to the doctor for his annual physical. Since one of his firm beliefs was "time is money," he always brought a specimen with him just so the examination would go faster. After checking him over and getting the lab tests back on the generous specimen McDuff had provided, the doctor assured the Scot he was in perfect health. That night at dinner McDuff was happy to announce that the lab report had shown that the news was good.

"Maggie," he said to his wife, "you'll be pleased to know that there's nothing wrong with you or me or our three bairns."

—•—

The old Scot lay dying. His relatives gathered around his bed to hear his last words. "I've been a hard man all my life," he admitted, "but I mean to go with a clear conscience. I owe Angus McGregor one hundred shillings."

"Ah, Doctor," said the old Scot's wife, "are you sure he's not in pain?"

"Quite sure," replied the doctor. "What makes you think that he's in pain?"

"Well, Doctor," she replied, "just listen to his delerious ramblings."

—•—

Two Scotsmen were discussing the son of a mutual friend who was going to medical school. "I understand young Sandy started out to be an ear specialist, but last term he switched over to dentistry. I wonder what made him change his mind?"

"I was talking to his father the other day, and I asked him that very question. He said it was a matter of arithmetic."

"They don't teach arithmetic in medical school!"

"No, but Sandy learned to count there. He told his father a man's got only two ears, but he's got thirty-two teeth, so you can see it's plainly a matter of arithmetic."

—•—

An old Scotsman was walking the moors with nothing for company but a bottle of very fine, very old, and very expensive whiskey tucked into his pocket. Suddenly he got his foot caught in a rut and found himself plunged forward into a ditch. He wasn't hurt, and so he picked himself up and resumed his walk. He hadn't gone but a few feet when he felt something trickling down his leg. "O Lord," he prayed, "please let it be blood."

SECRETARIES

You think your secretary is dumb? I asked mine to find me a number in the telephone book, and four hours later she still hadn't found it. I went out to her desk to see what was taking so long, and she told me not to worry and that she would have it in a few minutes. I asked her what made her think so, and do you know what she said? She said she was sure it wouldn't take much longer because she was up to the *L*'s already.

—•—

"Miss Jackson, you should have been here at nine o'clock!" bellowed her excited boss.

"Why," replied his gal Friday, "what happened?"

—•—

"I'm really worried," admitted Beth. "My boss says if I don't find ways to do my work faster, he's going to have to fire me."

"I just found out something the other day that really helps me save time," said her friend.

"What's that?" asked Beth.

"The dictionary is in alphabetical order."

—•—

"What are you looking for in a secretary?" asked the personnel director.

"Nothing much," replied the boss. "Just find me a secretary who looks like a girl, acts like a lady, thinks like a man, and works like a dog."

—•—

"How do you want these letters spaced?" inquired Mr. Jones's eager new secretary.

"I think you had better double-space them," he replied.

"Fine, sir," she said. "Now, how would you like the carbons spaced?"

—•—

"You know," said the office manager to her boss, "the typists around here are just like geiger counters."

"What do you mean?" inquired her boss.

"The closer I get, the faster they click."

SELF-MADE MAN

Two men met at the local barbershop and fell into conversation. Soon they discovered that they had a mutual acquaintance who happened to be one of the town's wealthiest men.

"You know," said one, "Fred Fisher is really a self-made man."

"That's true enough," admitted the second. "Trouble is, he worships his creator!"

SEX EDUCATION

Many parents believe in being open and aboveboard with their children, especially about sex, but I think one couple carried it too far. They took their six-year-old daughter to see one of those "adult" movies. She sat quietly in her seat until the couple on the screen worked their way into a very explicit clinch. It was then that a small voice carried through the theater: "Hey, Mommy, is this when he puts the pollen on her?"

—•—

"John," said Mrs. Martin, "do you think I should sign this permission slip Billy's teacher sent us?"

"What is it for, dear?"

"It will give him permission to attend a sex-education course three times a week."

"Well, he's growing up, you know. He'll have to know sometime."

"Oh, I'm not worried about that," she replied. "He knows already. It's just that I'm worried about the kind of homework he might have to do."

SHIPWRECKED

Two men, shipwrecked for weeks on a desert island, were passing the time playing a guessing game. The category they chose was movie stars. "I am five feet, six inches tall," said the first. "My measurements are thirty-six, twenty-two, thirty-six. My hair is blonde, my eyes are green, and I am noted for my roles as the sultry 'other woman' in many movies. Who am I?"

"Who cares?" cried his smitten companion. "Just kiss me."

SHOW BUSINESS

A brash film producer known more for his ability to raise money than for his artistic awareness happened to be on the set of his latest historical epic. He and the director were talking when an unfamiliar actor walked by.

"Who's he?" asked the producer.

"He's playing Napoleon," replied the director.

"Oh," said the skeptical producer, "do you think you should have such a short man play such an important part?"

—●—

You really *can't* please everybody, no matter how hard you try. Take the case of the tightrope walker who wanted to put together an act nobody had ever seen before. He had a rope stretched across the Grand Canyon, refused a net, had himself blindfolded, and then announced he would walk across the rope playing the "Blue Danube Waltz" on a violin. Needless to say, a huge crowd gathered to see this performance, but as he approached the far side of the canyon, this is the conversation he overheard.

"Now, admit it, Harry. Have you ever seen anything like that in your whole life? Isn't he amazing? Isn't he incredible?"

"Okay, I admit it," said Harry. "He's amazing. He's incredible. But I'll tell you one thing he isn't."

"And what's that?" asked his wife.

"Heifetz, he isn't."

—●—

A harried Broadway director was heard shouting the other day during the rehearsal of a genuine turkey, "Get me a ballet dancer!"

"Boss," asked one of his underlings, "what do you want with a ballet dancer? This play isn't even a musical."

"I know what this play isn't" came the pained reply, "but I just thought it would make me feel better if somebody around here was on his toes."

SKIERS

Despite warnings from much better skiers, a headstrong American who was skiing in Switzerland decided to make a solo run down a dangerous slope. He didn't make it and found himself floundering, but uninjured, in a deep crevasse. Hours later a rescue party found the crevasse and thinking to reassure the skier, shouted down, "We're from the Red Cross!"

"Sorry," called the proud American, "I gave at the office."

SOLDIERS

Two GI's were huddled together in a trench while the shells whizzed over their heads. One was very calm about the situation, but the other seemed extremely nervous.

The calm soldier said, "Don't worry, buddy, not one of those shells has our name on it."

"Yeah, I know that," replied his companion. "I'm worried about the ones marked 'To whom it may concern.' "

—●—

Two American Indians found themselves in a foxhole in Vietnam during a bombing raid. The ground exploded around them, and the sky was black with smoke.

"I thought that the war to end all wars had already been fought," said the first as he adjusted his helmet.

"Yes," replied the other, "but when they smoked the peace pipe afterward, nobody inhaled."

SPELLING

"My teacher is a bigot," said young Sally.

"Why, whatever makes you say that?" asked her mother.

"Well, she thinks that words should be spelled one way and one way only."

STATE OF THE WORLD

Sometimes I really wonder what the world is coming to. My son's teacher moonlights as a cabdriver. The cop in our neighborhood has a part-time job in a bowling alley. Everybody seems to be holding down two jobs. Never before in the history of mankind have so many worked so hard to be able to afford all the latest *labor-saving* appliances.

—•—

"Madam," said the clerk, "this is the perfect toy. Not only is it nontoxic and nonbreakable, but it is highly educational. The child who has this toy will gain real insight."

"Well, I don't know," replied the customer. "It looks awfully complicated to me."

"Don't worry, madam. That is the whole point. No matter how your child puts it together, it won't work."

—•—

"Tell me, Reverend," inquired a parishioner one Sunday after church. "They say young people are moving away from religion and yet your church is full of them. Why do you suppose that is?"

"Well," replied the world-weary churchman, "I suspect that after sowing all their wild oats on Saturday night they have to come to church to pray for crop failure."

—•—

One old-timer to another while watching a news broadcast: "You know, Zeke, when we were young, scientists all seemed to be puzzling over how old the world really is. Nowadays it seems they're all wondering about how old it's likely to get."

—●—

A lady called a TV repairman and asked him to rush right over and fix her set. "Tell me what the trouble is, lady," he said. "Maybe you just don't have it adjusted right."

"Well," she said, "I'm watching the six o'clock news, and the broadcaster has a very long face."

"Try another channel," replied the repairman. "You can't tell anything with newscasters. If you had to read those reports, you'd have a long face, too."

—●—

Mrs. Cohen and Mrs. Levy were overheard discussing world affairs.

"Tell me, Ceil," inquired Mrs. Levy, "what do you think of Red China?"

"To tell you the truth, Dolly," replied Mrs. Cohen, "on a yellow tablecloth it would look very nice."

STATISTICS

Statistics can be startling and often misleading. Take, for example, the case of a logging camp up north where there were one hundred men and only four women who were employed as cooks. Before the logging season was over, four of the men had married the cooks. However, statistically speaking, this meant that 4 percent of the men had married 100 percent of the women.

Two girls were having lunch. "You know," said one, thinking of some statistics she had just seen, "every time I breathe a man dies."

"Good grief," cried her friend, "why don't you use a mouthwash?"

STOCKS

"Tell me, dear," said his loving wife, "were you a bull or a bear in the market today?"

"I was a jackass."

STRATEGY

Fred was a middle-aged rooster who had been king of the barnyard for years. But lately egg production had been poor, and the hens were getting restless, so Farmer Brown felt it was time to replace Fred with a younger rooster. However, because of his long years of service, Farmer Brown decided to save Fred from the stew pot. Instead he decided to leave him in the barnyard as long as he didn't cause any trouble with the new rooster. Fred appreciated the gesture and greeted the new rooster with enthusiasm. Actually, it seemed as if he really wanted the new rooster to make good.

"Just so there won't be any question about who's in charge," said Fred to his replacement, "I have an idea that will establish your authority right away."

"Is that so?" replied the new rooster. "What's your plan?"

"Well," said Fred, "you give me a head start, and then you start chasing me around the barn. The hens will see me running away from you, and they'll think that I'm afraid of you, and that way they'll know who's boss."

"Sounds all right to me," said the young rooster. "Let's go."

So Fred took off, and a few seconds later the young rooster charged off after him, making a fearful racket. Suddenly Farmer Brown and his hired hand appeared in the barnyard, and seeing what was going on, Farmer Brown picked up the new rooster and wrung its neck.

"Can't understand it," said the farmer to his hired man. "This is the third new rooster this month, and every single one of them has been queer."

SUBSTITUTION

When Miss Lee, the contentious kindergarten teacher, decided to get married, it became necessary to find someone to replace her until she returned from her honeymoon. After much searching a substitute was found, and Miss Lee was able to go off content in the knowledge that a well-qualified teacher was taking care of her class. When she returned from her trip, she and her new husband decided to give a cocktail party to show their appreciation for the substitute teacher. However, the guests were more than a little shocked when the groom introduced the substitute teacher as "the kind lady who substituted for my wife during our honeymoon."

SUICIDE

"If I don't give in," said the wide-eyed young starlet, "would you really commit suicide?"

"Well," replied the jaded producer, "that is my *standard* procedure."

—●—

Young Jenny hadn't been at college three months when she suddenly appeared back home. "Now, Mama," said Jenny, "I might as well be honest. I'm going to have a baby."

Her mother seemed calm. "Jenny, I want you to promise me that you won't say a word about this to your father. He hasn't been well lately, and I'm afraid this might kill him."

"All right, Mama," said Jenny.

"And don't tell your brother. You know what a big mouth he has. The whole town will know if he finds out."

"If you say so," said Jenny. "But what about you, Mama? Don't you have anything to say?"

"No, dear, I'd never make a scene. I'm just going up to my room now and commit suicide."

SUPERSTITION

An amorous couple heard a noise in the living room of the lady's apartment. After slipping out of bed and peeking out, she turned and whispered fiercely, "Quick, get out! It's my husband." The man pulled his clothes on but realized he was trapped. "Jump," she urged. "Jump out the window."

"But we're on the thirteenth floor."

"This," she replied disgustedly, "is a fine time to be superstitious."

—●—

A traveling salesman stopped for the night in a small town in the hills of Tennessee. Before going to sleep he decided to go down to the bar and have a nightcap. While he was having his drink, he struck up a conversation with an attractive young lady, and after a few more drinks he invited her to accompany him back to his room. The girl was quite friendly and once inside started taking off her dress.

"Tell me, honey," said the salesman, "how old are you?"

"I'm thirteen years old," she replied with a smile.

"Good God!" cried the salesman, "get your clothes on and get out of here. You must think I'm crazy."

The girl gathered up her clothes and headed for the door. "Gee," she said sadly, "you shouldn't be so superstitious."

TEACHERS

"Why did you give up teaching?" asked Miss Jenkins's new boss.

"It's really quite simple," she replied. "In the school where I taught the teachers were afraid of the principal. The principal was afraid of the P.T.A. The parents in the P.T.A. were afraid of their kids. And the kids," she added sadly, "were afraid of no one."

TEXAS

I know a Texan who was so excited before his first child was born that when his wife developed a craving for mints, he tried to buy her Fort Knox.

—•—

I know a man from Texas who is so lazy that last year he gave his wife an oil well for Christmas just so he wouldn't have to wrap any presents.

—•—

I know one Texan who is so rich that he doesn't even bother to buy air-conditioned cars. He just keeps a couple of cold ones in his freezer.

TRAFFIC

In traffic court they have a new definition for the old expression "The quick and the dead." The quick are the ones who had time to get out of the way; the dead are the ones who didn't.

—•—

Judge: "You've been charged with doing 120 miles an hour in a 60-mile zone."

Defendant: "I just can't help it, your honor. I just seem to do everything in life fast."

Judge: "Really? Well, let's see how fast you can do sixty days."

—●—

A cop pulled a speeder over and proceeded to write out a ticket.

"You'll be sorry for this," said the speeder threateningly. "The traffic commissioner is a friend of mine."

"Well, that's just fine," replied the cop. "At least now he'll be sure I'm on the job."

—●—

One man-about-town I know was stopped by a policeman the other night for going through a traffic light. When the cop asked him why he didn't stop, he came up with quite a reason.

"Didn't you see the red light?" demanded the cop.

"Hell, no, officer," my friend exclaimed. "I didn't even see the *house*."

—●—

The police in this city are really cracking down on bad drivers. I know one guy who got fifty traffic tickets. He used to drive one of those fancy foreign sports cars, but the cops finally caught up with him, and they really let him have it. Not only did they take away his driver's license; they even deported his car.

—●—

A lady stopped for a red light only to have her car stall and block up one of the busiest intersections in town. She tried to get it started, but it was no use. The light turned green, then yellow, then red, but she couldn't move. Finally a harried traffic cop appeared on the scene and strode up to the car. "Tell me, lady," he said sarcastically, "ain't we got a color that suits you?"

TRAINS

"Did you get home all right last evening, sir?" asked the conductor.

"Yes," replied the commuter. "What makes you ask?"

"Well," replied the conductor, "last night you very graciously offered a lady your seat."

"But why should that make you wonder if I got home all right?"

"Because, sir, when you offered it to her, you were the only two people in the car."

TRIPLETS

A doctor who had just delivered triplets decided to give the new father the good news personally. He discovered that the man was out of town on a business trip, so he placed a long-distance call and waited for the operator to call him back. When the call came through, the doctor found himself talking to a chambermaid who was cleaning up the room.

"Let me talk to Mr. Stevens. I want to give him some news."

"He isn't available," replied the maid.

"Well," said the busy doctor, "would you please tell him that his wife has just given birth to triplets?"

"I'd rather not," she replied. "He's in the bathroom shaving."

TRUTH

A farmer gathered his six sons around him and demanded, "Which one of you boys pushed the outhouse into the creek?" The culprit did not step forward. "Now, boys," said the farmer, "remember the story of George Washington and the cherry tree. It's true that young George chopped down that tree, but he told his father the truth, and his father was proud of him." Whereupon the farmer's youngest son stepped forward and admitted that he had pushed the outhouse into the creek. The farmer picked up a switch and proceeded to whip his son soundly.

"But, Pa," protested the boy tearfully, "you told me that George Washington's father was *proud* of him when he confessed to chopping down the cherry tree."

"He was, son," replied the farmer, "but George Washington's father wasn't *sitting* in the cherry tree when his son chopped it down."

TURTLES

I just love animals. Everybody in my family loves animals. Every one of my kids has a pet of his own—all, that is, except my youngest son. It's a sad story. He used to have a turtle, but it passed away.

Poor thing fell in love with a souvenir German helmet I have and died of a broken heart.

UNDERSTANDING

"I wouldn't worry too much, Mr. Billings," said his exasperated secretary, "your wife isn't the only one. To tell you the truth, nobody around here understands you either."

UNDERTAKERS

During funeral services for old Mr. Willoughby the undertaker sidled up to Mrs. Willoughby and inquired, "How old a man was your husband?"

"Ninety-eight," replied his widow. "Two years older than me."

"My, my," replied the eager mortician, "hardly worth going home, is it?"

—●—

A man called the local undertaker and said, "This is Mr. Harvey. Would you please come up right away. I want you to supervise my wife's funeral."

"Certainly, sir," replied the undertaker. "Where do you live?"

"Seventeen Bowling Green Boulevard."

"But that is impossible," replied the undertaker. "I buried your wife three years ago."

"Yes, I know," replied Mr. Harvey, "but I've remarried."

"Well," replied the undertaker enthusiastically, "congratulations!"

VACATIONS

The day he returned from his vacation Bunsby asked his boss for two weeks off so he could get married and go on a honeymoon.

"For heaven's sake!" cried his exasperated employer, "why didn't you get married and go on your honeymoon during these past two weeks?"

"Are you kidding?" cried Bunsby. "And ruin my vacation!"

—●—

Mrs. Cantor was talking to an old friend she hadn't seen in years. There had always been a little friendly rivalry between the ladies, so

Mrs. Cantor was doing her level best to impress her friend. "You know," she said, "last year my Jake and I, we took a world cruise. Three months we was traveling, but this year we're going somewhere else."

—•—

An American playboy spent a weekend in England on a country estate. When he returned, he stopped off for a drink with his best friend.

"How was your weekend?" inquired his friend.

"Well," replied the playboy, "let's put it this way. If the soup had been as warm as the wine, the wine as old as the pheasant, the pheasant as sweet as the chambermaid, and the chambermaid as willing as my hostess, it would have been a marvelous weekend."

VANITY

Two old maids were walking home from church one Sunday morning. "Tell me, Ethel, what do you consider your worst sin?"

"Well," said Ethel, "I must admit my worst sin is vanity. I sit in front of the mirror for hours just admiring my beauty."

"I wouldn't worry too much," replied her friend. "That isn't vanity. It's just your imagination."

VIRTUE

A country vicar and a young actress found themselves seated together at a large dinner party. The conversation fell upon the changing morality of the times. The young actress took the part of the pragmatist, whereas the vicar upheld the old and virtuous ways.

"Let me ask you this, then, child," said the vicar. "Would you live with a man if he were to offer you, let us say, a million pounds?"

"Of course, I would. A girl would be a fool not to."

"Well, then, would you live with this same man if he offered you five pounds?"

"I would not!" came the outraged reply. "What kind of woman do you think I am?"

"My dear," replied the vicar, "we have already established the *kind* of woman you are. All that is left is to haggle over the price."

WAITERS

"Waiter! Look at this bowl of soup. It has a hair in it."
"No kidding?" said the waiter. "You better check the color. Our blonde waitress is missing."

—•—

After cutting into a bleeding steak which the waiter had ceremoniously plunked down in front of him, the customer snapped, "Didn't you hear me say 'Well done'?"
"I certainly did, sir," replied the waiter. "And may I say, sir, it's a pleasure to serve a man who appreciates me."

—•—

A man bit into a wiener and said to the waiter, "I think there is something wrong with these hot dogs."
"Don't tell *me* about it, Mac," replied the waiter. "I'm no veterinarian."

WATERMELON

Discovering too late that her teen-age son had used pure vodka to spike the watermelon she was serving to a group of churchmen, Mrs. Pruitt waited nervously for their reaction. To her amazement, however, not one of them had a single complaint. Her son, though, was not at all surprised.
"Gee, Mom," he said with a grin, "what did you expect them to say? They were all too busy stuffing the seeds in their pockets."

WEATHER

A weatherman predicted rain in no uncertain terms on his morning broadcast. After the show one of the station hands asked, "How come you're so positive it's going to rain today?"
"Simple," replied the weatherman. "I'm playing golf this afternoon, my wife is taking the three youngest kids on a picnic, and my oldest daughter is going to a garden party."

—•—

The weatherman at a local TV station was always wrong. As a matter of record he was wrong three hundred times last year. It got so bad that he became the laughingstock of the station and the community. He was so humiliated that he decided to quit and try another line of work. When he was filling out an application for a new job, he came across this question: "Reason for leaving last job?" His honest answer was "The climate never agreed with me."

—•—

My wife is so considerate you wouldn't believe it. She's always worrying about me and the kids. Can't do enough for us. Why, last fall she heard a weatherman say that we were in for a long, hard winter, and you know what she did? She rushed right out and bought a brand-new muffler for the car.

—•—

"I really couldn't say, buddy," said a very naïve husband to the man on the phone. "You'll have to call the weather bureau."

"Who was that?" inquired his wife as he hung up the phone.

"I don't know," he replied. "Just some guy who wanted to know if the coast was clear."

WEDDINGS

A rather confused elderly uncle accosted a young man dressed in a cutaway at an elaborate formal wedding and said, "Tell me, are you the young man who is marrying my niece today?"

"No, sir," replied the young man. "I was eliminated in the semifinals."

—•—

Two men were talking. "You look awfully worried, Bill," said his friend.

"I am," replied Bill. "I'm trying to decide if I really want to go to a wedding tomorrow."

"Why, who's getting married?" asked his friend.

"I am."

—•—

"Did you hear about the awful shock Ben got on his wedding day?" asked Maryjane.

"Sure!" replied Suellen. "I was at the wedding. *I* saw her, too."

—●—

"Why so glum?" inquired one of the ushers of the best man as they sat enjoying a postwedding drink.

"Oh, I was just thinking. The one thing that's wrong with being the best man at a wedding is that you never get a chance to prove it."

WELFARE

A welfare worker was interviewing a woman who was applying for assistance. "I see by your application that you have six children, Mrs. Stuart. How old is your youngest?"

"My youngest boy is six months old," she replied.

"But I also see by your application that your husband has been dead for five years. How do you explain that?"

"Well, sir, it's true that *he* died five years ago, but *I* didn't."

—●—

Little Freddy found himself out of money six days before his weekly allowance was due again, so he went to his father to see if there were any jobs around the house that might provide him with some spending money. His father couldn't think of a thing, and little Fred was at a loss until he thought of the perfect solution. He asked his father to put him on welfare.

WIGS

"I'd give anything for so much as a lock of Cynthia's hair," said the love-struck young man.

"Well, if you give me twenty bucks," replied his sister, "I can get you the whole thing. I know where she bought it."

WISDOM

Overheard in a Sunday school class:
"Why was King Solomon considered the wisest man in the world?"
"Probably because he had so many wives to tell him what to do."

—●—

"Tell me, Guru," said the young man, "if you were locked in a room with the most beautiful woman in the world, would you be able to resist temptation?"

"Of course," replied the holy man, "but what would be the point?"

"I don't understand," said the young man.

"My meaning is this. I *know* I can resist temptation, but can the rest of the world resist the urge to *slander* me?"

—•—

A young reporter was interviewing old Harry Blackwell on his 101st birthday. "Tell me, Mr. Blackwell, if you had your life to live over again, would you still make the same mistakes?"

"Sure as hell would" came his emphatic reply.

"You mean you wouldn't do *anything* differently?"

"Sure would. I'd start sooner."

WOMEN

That woman really knows how to hurt a guy. She was the one who introduced her husband to her psychiatrist at a cocktail party by saying, "Doctor, I want you to meet my husband. He's one of the men I've been telling you about."

—•—

Why is it that science can tell that man is millions of years old but that no man can find out just how old any one woman really is?

—•—

A man started across the street as the light turned green and was very nearly run down by a woman driving a station wagon full of children. The man leaped back just in time and hollered angrily, "Lady, don't you know when to stop?"

Looking back at the car full of kids and then at him, she declared in a very cold tone, "They're not all mine."

—•—

Two men were discussing women. "Now you take this Sophia Loren," said the first. "What's she got that's so great? You take away her beautiful hair, her smooth skin, her fabulous body, and what have you got?"

"My wife" was the sad reply.

—●—

A newly engaged secretary was so annoyed when no one in her office noticed her ring that she was moved to exclaim in a loud voice, "My, it's warm in here. I think I'll take off my ring."

—●—

"My husband is just nuts about me," cooed a sweet young thing to her mother. "He even talks about me in his sleep, and he says such nice things even if he does keep calling me by the wrong name."

—●—

"Darling," said Nellie to her unsuspecting spouse, "is it true that money talks?"

"That's what they say, dear."

"Well, in that case how about leaving me a hundred dollars? I get *so* lonely."

—●—

Around midnight the desk sergeant answered a call at the precinct, and an excited woman said, "A man just broke into my apartment."

"Now, keep calm, lady," said the sergeant. "What does he look like?"

There was a long pause while the lady examined the intruder. "Well, he's about six two, he has black curly hair, broad shoulders, nice white teeth, and a beautiful smile. And I want you to be sure and have him out of my apartment by nine o'clock tomorrow morning."

—●—

There's only one thing that can *really* separate the men from the boys. *Women!*

—●—

A very well-to-do middle-aged lady was having her portrait painted. She and the artist became quite friendly, and when he completed the portrait, she said, "I have something I'd like you to do for me because I feel I can trust you."

"Anything, my dear lady," he said.

"I really do admire your work," she said, "but I would like it if you would make a few additions to my portrait."

"I don't think I follow you," replied the artist.

"I would like you to paint a magnificent diamond necklace around my neck, a beautiful pair of ruby earrings on my ears, and a huge emerald ring on my finger."

"Whatever for?" asked the artist.

"Well," she replied sadly, "I married a much younger man, and I know now that he married me only for what little money I have, and I know he's been seeing another woman. I even know that they are planning to kill me, and their plan is so clever that if I were to try to resist or accuse them of attempting such a crime, I would probably be forced to spend the rest of my days in an asylum."

"Dear lady, this is terrible," said the horrified artist. "Is there nothing I can do?"

"Just do as I ask. Paint the jewelry on the portrait."

"But whatever for?"

"Because there isn't any jewelry, and when I'm gone, I want my husband's new wife to go crazy looking for it."

—•—

A not-so-dumb blonde found herself at a cocktail party in Dallas. Never one to miss an opportunity, she turned to the Texan at her side and said, "Pleased to meet you, honey. How much did you say your name was?"

—•—

A doctor was visiting the maternity clinic one morning. As he went from bed to bed, the nurse would inform him of the expectant mother's probable delivery date. He noticed that the first three ladies were all going to have their babies on February 18. As they were approaching the fourth woman's bed, the doctor said, "Tell me, nurse, is this lady expecting her baby on February eighteenth, too?"

"I really couldn't say," admitted the nurse. "I don't think she was at the picnic."

—•—

A pretty young girl stopped into the neighborhood bookshop and bought a dictionary. The clerk who sold it to her was smitten, so you can imagine how pleased he was when she stopped in again a few days later.

"How do you find your dictionary?" he asked, thinking to start a conversation.

"It's very interesting," she assured him. "Only it's very hard to read because of the way it keeps changing the subject."

—•—

Lady lawyer: "And what is your age, madam?"
Lady witness: "About the same as yours."

—•—

A man decided to surprise his wife by giving her a horse for her birthday. One Saturday morning he went to a nearby stable and told the old horse trader who ran the place what he had in mind. There were several horses for sale. One in particular caught the man's eye, but he hesitated because the horse seemed a little wild. "Tell me, old-timer, could a woman handle that horse?"

The horse trader thought for a minute and replied, "A woman *could* handle that horse. But I sure wouldn't want to be the guy she was married to."

—•—

"Helen, I've got to fire that new chauffeur you hired. He's nearly killed me five times this week, and it isn't even Friday."

"Don't be too hasty, dear," replied his mate. "Let's give him one more chance."

—•—

Overheard in a crowded restaurant: "All right, John, I *admit* that I love to spend money, but just you name me one *other* extravagance."

—•—

"Darling, of course I *spend* more than you make. But it's only because I have such confidence in you!"

—•—

I know you've all heard the old joke that behind every great man there stands a woman who had *nothing* to wear. Well, don't you believe it. Behind every great man there stand two women: his proud wife and his flabbergasted mother-in-law.

—•—

Mr. and Mrs. Mason were having a slight difference of opinion. "It is obvious that I am right," snapped Mrs. Mason. "After all, since God created woman second, we must be an improvement on the original model."

"Actually, my dear, He created woman second because He didn't want any advice."

—•—

"Tell me, Senator, do you believe in clubs for women?"

"Oh, yes," replied the senator. "But only if all other means of persuasion fail."

—•—

Myrtle arrived home with the front of the car all smashed and dented. Naturally, her husband was enraged. "At least," sobbed Myrtle, "my own husband could be as nice as the policeman who reported the accident. He asked me if I'd like the city to take down all the telephone poles."

—•—

"Darling, I had a little accident on the way home tonight, but don't worry, I just scratched the fender."

"I'll go have a look at it."

"Fine, dear, it's in the back seat."

—•—

"Tell me," demanded a newly converted women's libber of her boyfriend, "do you like smart women?"

"Well," he replied, "I like a girl with a good head on my shoulder."

WRITERS

Author to critic: "What is your opinion of my new novel?"
Critic: "It's worthless!"
Author: "I know. But I'd like it anyway."

—●—

Overheard at a cocktail party for a famous author: "Oh, Mr. Farnsworth, I've been dying to meet you. Why, just the other day I was reading something of yours about one thing or another in some magazine."

—●—

A famous writer spoke to a group of students and then agreed to answer any questions.

"Tell me, sir," asked one student, "where did you get the idea for the plot of your second novel?"

"Actually," replied the author with a smile, "I got it from the film version of my first."

ZIPPERS

A very fat lady boarded a crowded bus and managed to wedge herself in. She had a long way to go and feeling very uncomfortable, reached down and unzipped the zipper in the back of her skirt. A few minutes later, feeling a draft, she reached back and zipped it up again. Feeling more and more uncomfortable, she reached back and unzipped the zipper, but in a few minutes she reached back and zipped herself up again. This went on for nearly twenty minutes until finally the man standing behind her leaned over and said, "Listen, lady. I don't know what's on your mind, but in the last half hour you've unzipped my fly at least ten times!"